HEAR ME NOW
Audition Monologues
for Actors of Colour

Edited by Titilola Dawudu
and Tamasha Theatre Company

methuen | drama
LONDON • NEW YORK • OXFORD • NEW DELHI • SYDNEY

METHUEN DRAMA
Bloomsbury Publishing Plc
50 Bedford Square, London, WC1B 3DP, UK
1385 Broadway, New York, NY 10018, USA
29 Earlsfort Terrace, Dublin 2, Ireland

BLOOMSBURY, METHUEN DRAMA and the Methuen Drama logo
are trademarks of Bloomsbury Publishing Plc

First published in Great Britain by Oberon Books 2018
This edition published by Methuen Drama 2022

Cover image: Malikah K Holder @emkayhaytch
Text design: Konstantinos Vasdekis

A catalogue record for this book is available from the British Library.

A catalog record for this book is available from the Library of Congress.

ISBN: PB: 978-1-3502-9160-7
ePub: 978-1-7868-2462-2

Printed and bound in Great Britain

eBook conversion by Lapiz Digital Services, India.

To find out more about our authors and books visit www.bloomsbury.com
and sign up for our newsletters.

CONTENTS

Foreword
by Titilola Dawudu

Hear Me Now is about legacy. I think about who this can be passed onto and how it will make a difference. This journey started eight or nine years ago when I started writing audition monologues for the young black actors I was working with. I have been mentoring black, mainly female actors and theatre-makers for years and have been aware that there has been a struggle to find relevant material to go into an audition with or use in workshops. When I did my MA in 2014 at Central Saint Martins, I spoke to the very few black actors and directors at the university and found that we were still having the same conversations.

After approaching Fin Kennedy and Debo Adebayo at Tamasha, who also had a similar concept at the time, I knew there was a space for this idea and *Hear Me Now* was born. This project saw writers of colour work with actors of colour to come up with audition monologues that spoke to them. What is unique and the most important element of this collection is that the voices of the actors are heard; we have an astronaut preparing to be the first black man on the moon, a mother telling her son that she is in love with a woman, a boy whose dinner lady encourages him to learn how to read, a single dad baking cupcakes with his young daughter, a nun in love with her priest...and so on. Rich, new, complexed, layered voices.

As a writer who is black, my name would often be followed by the word 'emerging'. I saw this as a hindrance as too many writers and actors of colour are being described as this and our work is too often seen at scratch nights rather than the professional stages. Who decides who is emerging – and for how long? I wanted to enable writers who are of colour to have their work in the pages of a book, to be read, to be acted out, to be in the hands of many, many people, to be on bookshelves, to be worn-out and overused. The writers in this book will not just have one moment to shine, but endless moments.

Deciding to use the term 'of colour' brought up different conversations with different people. It can be as problematic as Black, Asian, Minority Ethnic (BAME), but I took inspiration from Loretta Ross and the activists in the seventies and I'm using it as solidarity between the underrepresented voices of writers and actors of colour within the arts industry. We're still fighting to be heard, aren't we? We're still missing from the stage and we are still missing in leadership and behind the scenes. I hope that we can find ourselves in this collection. Actors – I want this book to be for you. I want you to find yourself in here. Explore, discover, embrace.

I am proud to share this space with others who are changing how things are being done and creating legacies; I believe there is room for us all, we just have to hear each other. Now.

Foreword

by Noma Dumezweni

Hear Me Now. Many voices are growing. I see 'representation' being demanded. A time to share one's lived experience in the form of Storytellers, Writers and Actors. Now this may seem obvious of any monologue book, but the truth is I've never come across a collection written only by people of varying ages and of colour. All. Of. Colour.

You may not think this is for you. But I feel that if you are a storyteller in word, speech, movement and emotion, have a peek. These are of shared experiences. Whatever form they are in. They are human stories.

Hear Me Now. In Rachel Coombe's 'Ace of Clubs' – I know those feelings. In Yasmeen Khan's 'Broken' – I acknowledged those fears. In 'Nashville' by Rabiah Hussain – I was saluting Nikita's choice, amidst the many running through her. These are characters amongst many in the book that I want to experience and see what my version of them would be. You don't have to do much, just play with them. Exploring feeling and sharing...your version.

Hear Me Now. This book of monologues exists because people didn't hear their voices. And now they've made their seats to put at the table. To share with others. They are for you. To create. To imagine. And therefore to experience. For you. Just. Play.

Thank You

A huge thank you to all the actors involved who were imperative in making this collection what it is. It's your voices in these stories that will be used for other actors. Thank you for being a part of this legacy.

Reaching Higher

Bukola Garry
Leanne Henlon
Mark Hobbs
Tyrese Hudson
Tatenda-Naomi Matsvai

Ruth Olorunnisomo
Shaquille Proud
Kaylem Shepherd
Shayde Sinclair

Tamasha workshops

Adil Akram
Iman Boujelouah
Charlotte Burke
Tahira Dar
Naomi Denny
Megha Dhingra
India Eva-Rae
Chris Fung
Annie Jaffri Rahman
Gunalp Kocak
Danielle Kolanis
Sanjay Lago
Vinay Lad
Alice Langrish
Nyla Levy
Sophia Lockhart
Abner Motaung

Zisha Nafsar
Dixita Pandya
Vicky Pasion
Amer Patel
Andrea Ortiz
Ruchi Ranjan
Roshni Rathore
Kal Sabir
Raagni Sharma
Shiv Sharma
Zainab Shofolahan
Harriet Smithers
Alan Suri
Ana Torre
Joyce Veheary
Minhee Yeo

National Youth Theatre

Seraphina Beh
Chinenye Ezeudu
Daisy Fairclough
Shiv Jalota

Shalisha James-Davis
Joshua Lyster-Downer
Kwami Odoom
Nathaniel Wade

**Rightful Place Theatre
(formerly Mulberry Alumni
Theatre Company)**

Ferdous Ahmed

Rukshana Amer

Afsana Begum

Rashma Begum

Tania Hossain

Sabina Khan

Bahar Khanam

Rubaiyath Reza

Nowshin Sweety

Shakela Tariq

Company Three

Michael Adewale

Doyin Ajiboye

Yaamin Chowdhury

Ned Glasier

Romeo Mika

Jake Monib

Abigail Phillips-Douglas

Pia Richards-Glöckner

Syntyche Tongomo

Segen Yosef

Purple Moon Drama

Nicole Abraham

Yinka Awoni

Antonia Elson

Daniel Francis-Swaby

Valerie Isaiah Sadoh

Nicholas Marrast-Lewis

Cheryl Ndione

Stephanie Stevens

Nicola Maisie Taylor

Generations Arts

Adrienne Bailey

Idris Balogun

Lily Barrow

Elena Burciu

Ali Godfrey

Sonia Gwynn

Jay Martin

Ike Nwachukwu

Tania Nwachukwu

Robert O'Reilly

Kyrae Patterson

Zachary Spooner

Also, thank you to Mina Barber, Bushra Laskar and Yasmin Hafesji for their dramaturgical support and Rikki Beadle-Blair.

tamasha

Tamasha means 'commotion', creating a stir. We have a 30 year proven history of reaching new writing audiences and specialise in making new work for the stage inspired by the ever-changing cultures of contemporary Britain. We aim to spark distinctive social discourse through compelling theatre experiences that place the voices of emerging and established artists from culturally diverse backgrounds centre-stage.

Landmark productions include *East Is East* (1996), *A Fine Balance* (2006), *Snookered* (2012), *My Name is...* (2014), *Blood* (2015), and *Made In India* (2017), winning acclaim from audiences and critics alike.

Alongside our national tours, Tamasha continues to nurture the next generation of theatre-makers through Tamasha Developing Artists; a national artist development programme with a track record of providing high-quality training and tangible professional opportunities for emerging and established theatre artists throughout their careers. We facilitate theatre-makers to engage with communities, young people and audiences through unique engagement, education projects and creative collaborations.

www.tamasha.org.uk
@tamashatheatre
www.facebook.com/tamashatheatre

Foreword
by Fin Kennedy, Artistic Director

In 2014, shortly after starting as Tamasha's Artistic Director, I set up an in-house writers' group, Tamasha Playwrights. I am myself a playwright and have taught for many years on Playwriting Masters degrees, including the MA Dramatic Writing at Central Saint Martins where I first met Titi Dawudu. Tamasha Playwrights was a consolidation of these years of experience into a professional preparation programme at Tamasha for eight writers of colour per year, in the form of an attachment scheme lasting an academic year. The freedom to do so outside of an academic programme of study was liberating. Tamasha Playwrights is not a taught course but a writer-led collective, in which every session is by majority demand from that year's participants. We offer sessions on the craft of playwriting itself, but also training in fundraising and self-producing, and teaching playwriting in schools and youth theatres – skills to sustain writers between commissions. There is also the space to suggest projects which the group can lead on with Tamasha's support – which is where *Hear Me Now* came from. Tamasha Playwrights is as much a nursery for new projects for Tamasha and its community of artists as it is about training writers.

As is often the case with good ideas, we were not the only ones to think of it. Great minds think alike, and when Titi Dawudu approached us with a very similar idea about writing better quality audition material for actors of colour, it made sense to join forces.

I'm not sure any of us expected the way the project would snowball. After an initial R&D phase with the National Youth Theatre, we held a scratch night presenting the first eight pieces at Rich Mix – and the audience reception around the need for this project was overwhelming. We were clearly onto something.

The workshop itself is very simple. It brings actors and writers together in one-to-one relationships; the actor develops a character they know they could play but would never get seen for, and the writers write a three minute speech in the voice of that character. A session plan for this workshop, a character worksheet, and some notes on successful monologue writing, are included in this book, to support groups or individuals to run their own *Hear Me Now* workshops independently (though let us know if you do – we might be able to help).

From this simple idea some truly wonderful characters emerged, from a cross-dressing imam, to the first black Prime Minister, to a devout Christian hit woman. A further iteration with slightly older actors via the Tamasha Developing Artists network confirmed our hunch that if we can empower actors of colour with powerful, fresh, funny, stereotype-busting audition material, we could increase their chances of being considered for roles outside of those they are usually offered. In time, this might change the nature of the representations of diverse communities we see on our stages and screens.

Tamasha supported Titi in a successful Arts Council funding bid to run the project in five different young people's companies in inner city areas across London over a whole year; she turned out to be a skilled producer and project manager as well as talented playwright. We are indebted to her for leading on the project with such skill and professionalism. We are delighted to share the 80+ pieces so far in this anthology, and hope that they empower actors in the UK and beyond to fully showcase their range to casting directors, agents and others. We are grateful to Oberon for taking the publication on, to RADA for hosting its launch, to Rich Mix for free space, to the actors and writers who gave so generously their time in the early stages and to the Arts Council for taking a leap of faith that this could really work.

Who knows where the *Hear Me Now* journey might lead next? Both Titi and Tamasha are curious about whether a longer show might emerge from the extraordinary and unexpected characters in the volume (some R&D has already taken place). We'd like to continue the project with other focuses, for example holding workshops outside London, or a volume focusing on disability. Watch this space...and if one of the pieces in this book lands you a great part, let us know! That kind of evidence is very useful for fundraising for further iterations.

They say there is nothing so powerful as an idea whose time has come. You, the readers and users of this volume now carry that idea. Use it, share it, make a noise about it - be heard, now. Your voice matters.

<u>Hear Me Now Session Plan</u>

A playwright-led workshop for actors, to develop diverse new audition pieces.

Session length:	2 hours 30 mins
Group size:	(Up to) 20 actors, 10 writers, 1 facilitator
Age range:	16+
Room:	Workshop space large enough for 30 people to move around in comfortably.
Materials needed:	1 large flipchart with at least 20 pages
	20 marker pens
	Blue tack
	Ballpoint pens for all participants
	Post-it notes
	Watch/stopwatch for facilitator
	Printed character questionnaires x 20 (see below)
	Character prompts (for facilitator use only)

Aims

By the end of the session participants will have:

- Communicated to their playwrights the distinct challenges they face in finding suitable audition pieces.
- Developed 5-10 ideas (per actor) for unusual new characters for whom a monologue might be written to suit the actor.
- Developed in sufficient depth one of those characters for the playwright to write a 3-min monologue for.
- Developed some understanding of the elements of successful dramatic storytelling in monologue form.

Mins	Exercise	Notes
0-10 mins	Intro from facilitator and purpose of session/project. Full group physical warm-up/ice breaker game.	Led by facilitator
10-30 mins	Improv in pairs: • 2 mins to rehearse up a short sketch: an actor leaving the worst audition of their life and unloading to their best mate about it. • Watch some back.	Led by facilitator
30-40 mins	Full group discussion responding to 3 questions: • What characters do you find you are type cast as? • What character types are you tired of seeing in theatre, TV or film? • What is your dream role?	Led by facilitator
40-70 mins	In threes (1 writer, 2 actors): • Tell each other your life story in one minute, then: • Decide on the most interesting life story of the three. • As a group, embellish it so it is even more dramatic. • Change the name to make it a character. • Decide who will tell it (not the person whose story it is based on). As full group: • Hear up to 10 x 1-min semi-fictional life stories. Discussion: What have we learned about short form solo storytelling from this exercise? What works, what doesn't? What lessons can we learn for writing pieces for a 3-min audition.	Led by facilitator

Mins	Exercise	Notes
70-75 mins	BREAK	
75-90 mins	Actors work individually to: • Come up with at least 5 (and ideally 10) rough character ideas involving 3 facts (name, age, job) and one surprise e.g. 'Dave, 35, plumber, loves ballet'. Remind them that these characters are about avoiding stereotypes. • Actors list these on A1 paper on the floor, one sheet each. • **Make sure they are all characters each actor might actually want to play (so an age range suited to each actor)** • After 10 mins or so, writers join in and look over the character ideas on the Actor's sheets. (The grouping of three should be the same as previously for the life story in one minute exercise). • In conversation with their writer, each actor decides on one character they are going to develop in more depth for the rest of the session. Writers can give a steer on the most promising ones. Actors can also introduce their character to one another within their groups.	Led by facilitator with writers observing at first, joining later.

Mins	Exercise	Notes
90-110 mins	All actors together (but individually): • Each actor finds a space and sits with eyes closed. • Facilitator leads a visualisation exercise in picturing the character, finding their look, energy, walk, voice as move around space. • Questions prompt biographical details (see facilitator prompts below).	Led by facilitator, writers sit out.
110-140 mins	In threes (but individually): • Each actor fills in a Character Questionnaire (see below) with details about the character they just created.	Actor-led, supported by writers
140-150 mins	Full group plenary / evaluation.	Led by facilitator

Notes and reminders for facilitator

Ensure all completed Character Questionnaire sheets are collected in and given to the writers. This is the main record they will have of the Actor's character idea.

Once groups of three are established for the 'life story in one minute' exercise, keep these groups throughout the workshop so that the writers write for these actors. Give each group one post-it note to write all three email addresses onto – the facilitator can then connect them after the session so the writers can ask the actors any questions they have as they develop the character's speech.

Remind the group about what happens next and the second workshop date, usually around 6 weeks later to give the writers time to do up to three drafts of the speech. The second workshop is not structured, it is just time for the writers and actors to reconvene so the actors can perform their piece in front of the writer and agree any final changes. It's also a nice opportunity for the group to watch each other's pieces in the final hour.

Character prompts for facilitator

Take these slowly – allow time for the questions to land and the actors to respond in their minds. This is a creative process so shouldn't be rushed. Ask the actors to close their eyes during it, and sit or lie down as they prefer. They should be comfortable. There should be no background noise or interruptions.

Visualise your character in your mind's eye – they are standing facing you. What do they look like? Zoom in, zoom out. Spin them 360 degrees.

- Are they male, female, neither, both?
- What is their face shape?
- Height?
- Body shape?
- Hair colour?
- Eye colour?
- Skin colour?
- The clothes they're wearing.
- What's the expression on their face as they look back at you
- Spin 360 degrees in your mind's eye
- How they're positioned – standing, sitting, lying, walking.

Biographical

- Where did they grow up? London? Another city? A town? A village? Another country? Have they moved away or do they still live there?
- How do they feel about where they grew up?
- Who brought them up? Parents? Grandparents? Siblings? Someone else?

- What kind of school did they go to? Did they enjoy it? What were their favourite subjects? Were they academic, sporty, popular, nerdy, which clique did they belong to – or did they do their own thing?
- At what age did they finish education? If they're still studying, what subject? If they went out to work – as what?
- What age are they now? (REMEMBER they need to be of an age where you the actor at the age you are now could realistically play them).
- Picture the accommodation they live in at the moment: house, flat, hostel, halls of residence?
- Who do they live with? Family, friends, flatmates, strangers, alone?
- What do they do for a living? Do they work – if so, as what? Full-time, part-time? Do they like it? Have they started a career of some kind of are they in casual jobs they don't much care about?
- If they aren't in paid employment, how do they fill their days? Studying? Parenting? Something else?
- What hopes do they have for the future?

Personality

- What personality type are they – confident and outgoing or shy and introverted? Do they follow their head or their heart? Are they impulsive, passionate, quick tempered – or thoughtful, reflective and careful?
- What kind of friends do they have? What do their friends think about them?
- What skills do they have – think of something they're really good at.
- What do they do for fun – are they sporty, booky, into music, pets, DIY. What unusual hobby might they have?
- What are their parents like? Are they still alive? Do they get on with them?

- Who else is an important figure in their lives? Someone who has really influenced how they see the world.
- Think about the kinds of things they believe in – religion, politics, sport, other people, themselves. What kinds of issues do they feel strongly about?
- Imagine meeting them for the first time. Where do you meet them? How do they introduce themselves? What does their voice sound like? What else do they say to you? Do you like them and think you'll get on with them or are they more detached, withdrawn or even cold?
- Imagine them at a party. Think about the energy they give off. What colour is it?

So now you know a bit about this person. You've pictured their physical appearance, you know about where they grew up, their personality type and their current situation in life.

Picture that situation. Imagine their average week, from Monday to Sunday.

How do they feel by the end of it? Happy, bored, frustrated, excited?

Think about something they lack in their life. Something which makes them feel unfulfilled.

Think about something they want, really really badly. Something they would take a big risk to try to get....

What are they doing right at this moment

- It's 7.30pm on a Tuesday evening (or whatever the actual time and date of the workshop).
- Where are they? At home? At college? Working late? Indoors/outdoors? On public transport? Where are they going? Are they socialising? Where – with who?
- Picture that scene... where they are, what they're doing.

Ask the actors to open their eyes

- Now show us them in that scene – take on the physicality of your character – stand, sit, walk as they are right this moment, at 7.30pm on a Tuesday evening.
- All of a sudden they get up. They start to walk. Use the whole space. Show us how they walk – is it confident and strong, or shy and inward?
- Where are they going?
- Find the part of the body they lead with when they walk.
- Think what status level they are from 1 to 10. Show us that status in their walk.
- As you pass each other as your character, start to acknowledge one another as your character would. Do they nod, wink, smile, speak?
- Start to acknowledge one another as you pass.
- Stop and have a chat.

FREEZE

Ask the actors to come out of character and form a line in front of the facilitator, to collect a Character Sheet. They can now sit and fill this in.

Character sheet

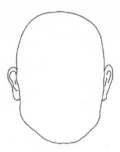

1. Name ....

2. Age ....

3. Job (or where their money comes from) ....

4. Star sign (plus the characteristics which most apply)
   ....

5. What sort of accommodation they live in ....
   ....

6. Three things they love:
   a) ....
   b) ....
   c) ....

7. Three things they hate:
   a) ....
   b) ....
   c) ....

8. Three things they'd buy (or do) if they won the lottery
   (NOT including house, car or holiday)
   a) ....
   b) ....
   c) ....

9. A phrase they over use ....

10. A secret they have ....
    ....

11. A problem they have ....
    ....

12. A happy memory ....
    ....

13. A sad memory ....
    ....

14. Something they believe strongly ....
    ....

15. Something they lack in their life ....
    ....

16. What they are doing at this very moment
    ....

17. What they are thinking or saying at this very moment
    ....
    ....

18. Someone or something which is a big influence upon them
    ....

19. A contradiction about them
    ....

20. A question you would like to ask them
    ....

Anything else?
    ....
    ....
    ....

Tips for writing a killer 3-minute monologue

We've learned a lot about writing monologues during the *Hear Me Now* process.

A monologue should be thought of as an interesting 'three-minute moment' in which to catch the character. You've only got three minutes so make every second count – it should be an important three minutes in the character's life, not just another day.

It helps to consider where they are, and the situation they are in at the time of speaking. This helps keep the speech in the present tense. Telling a story from the past, even the recent past, is pretty deathly to a monologue – because then it becomes literary rather than theatrical, told rather than shown. Theatrical monologues need to have a live, present tense situation which the character is grappling with. This situation should play out over the course of the speech, with some kind of change taking place in the character during it – making a decision, for example, or having some kind of realisation. There are some great examples from the *Hear Me Now* canon, all featured in this book:

In *Nashville* by Rabiah Hussain, Nikita is backstage awaiting her turn to perform at the country music version of X Factor, reflecting on how she got here and thinking about possibly pulling out.

In *I Dream Of Drake* by Tara Alexis, Charlene openly shares her most intimate hopes and fears with a sleeping lover, going back into herself once he wakes.

In *Douglas* by Mahad Ali, a black Prime Minister addresses the House of Commons having just declared a state of emergency.

In *James*, by Mediah Ahmed, a young man plucks up the courage to tell his strict Nigerian father that he wants to be a professional dancer, rehearsing what he will say in front of his bedroom mirror, with dad having just arrived downstairs.

It's also important to consider who the character is speaking to. Many of the monologues in this volume cast the audience as a character within the speaker's story – a best friend, rival, boss, client, journalist, police or a lover. Or, there might be some other reason for speaking such as recording a voicemail or a Skype video call, or rehearsing what they are about to say to someone they are expecting. It is usually less successful for a character to just start confessing all to no one in particular, and for no particular reason – after all, no one does this in real life. There are sometimes exceptions. When the writing is of top quality and the character particularly engaging, as in *Gold Dust* by Ross Willis, or *A Consecrated Love* by Mr Ekow, you can sometimes get away with it.

Three minutes is not a long time and it's easy to over-write. Less is more. You can think of it as three paragraphs of one minute each – beginning, middle, end. You need to hit the ground running and be clear from the outset who the character is and what situation they are in. The middle adds some detail or complication. And by the end some kind of change has taken place – however small.

Here are some other tips:

Give your character a strong want. This is where the Character Sheet comes in handy. What life stage are they at, and what do they still lack? Sometimes they can want something from the unseen person they are speaking to. What obstacles stand in their way, and how do they negotiate these over the course of the speech?

Something should be at stake. Your character should stand to gain or lose something significant, their life path somehow affected, by the outcome of whatever situation we find them in. This is what makes us want to keep watching.

Map the emotional and psychological states. Be clear about the different states the character moves through, and how these mirror the story. In *Welcome To The Good Life* by Bisola

Elizabeth Alabi, Emily is living in her car when her colleague Tom approaches. She goes from chatty and upbeat, in an attempt to cover the truth, to desperately trying to turn the conversation onto something else, until it finally becomes clear Tom has brought some cash from a whip round in the office, at which point she crumples, broken and ashamed, and pleads with him not to tell anyone else about her situation. Being clear about these states and their logical progression can really support the telling of a story in a short space of time.

Opening hook. A well-chosen first line can do a lot of work for you, from grabbing your audience's attention, establishing intrigue, to making it clear where we are and who we are with.

"I ... I can't believe we just did that."
(*Don't Say Anything* by Ayesha Manazir Siddiqi)

"I'm sorry I'm late, the traffic was a nightmare. Has my Assistant taken care of you?"
(*The Right Representation* by Karla Williams)

"I've spent the last six years thinking about this exact moment."
(*Sheen* by Safaa Benson-Effiom)

"This is my second time watching someone die."
(*My Father's Son* by Femi Keeling)

"Miles, this isn't the time for kissing."
(*Sheila* by Iman Qureshi)

'Button' closing. A satisfying closing line for your actor to land on – not necessarily resolving everything, but something the rest of the speech has been building up to, which perhaps encapsulates its themes in some way.

Sensory detail. It can be quite evocative for the character to mention smells, tastes, sounds, and these can come to life in the audience's mind quite vividly, certainly more so than descriptions of abstract things. They can also convey emotion in a subtle way.

Internal obstacles. All characters in dramatic narratives face obstacles, usually (though not always) the opposition of another character. Monologues provide a rare opportunity, through their confessional nature, to externalise the internal and show characters grappling with internal obstacles – fear, confusion, lack of knowledge or confidence. As with all dramatic writing it is better to show this in action through the character's behaviour than to describe it literally.

Give them something to do. Physical tasks which a character is engaging in as they speak are useful for your actor in performance. In *The Race* by Mina Barber, Mark is a trainee astronaut at NASA doing a press interview. The journalist asks him to pose on the treadmill which he switches on and runs on for the duration of the speech, steadily getting faster and faster as the interview itself spins out of his control. Physical tasks can work on a metaphorical level too.

Avoid back story. Of all the art forms, drama is the one most located in the present tense. Audiences only really care about what is taking place on stage in front of them right now. A character's back story is a lot less useful than many writers think. It might be useful to know it in order to write the character convincingly, but the audience don't need to hear it. In any case, a general sense of the life they have lived should be obvious from their energy, language and demeanour. Make sure that the speech itself remains mostly focused on the present tense situation they are currently in.

Long-held desires. Several of the speeches in this book find a character at a moment where they have finally acted on a long-held secret longing. It is always interesting to watch a character break free of their everyday existence and strike out into the unknown.

Comedy. Everyone likes a laugh – and in an audition this can be unexpected and delightful, and will ensure the casting director remembers you. Humour is your friend. Use it.

THE MONOLOGUES

A Consecrated Love
Mr Ekow

> **A nun who is in love with an older priest.
> For ages 18 to 30.**

Lost in your eyes, I almost dropped the collection plate
as you passed it to me. *(Sigh.)* Those eyes. At times
I think it's just in my head, but then we keep having
these wild encounters. Like that time I was handing out
the hymn sheets and your hand 'accidentally' rubbed
against mine – it was electric! Plus it gave me enough
time to see you're the only man here without a wedding
ring. And here we meet again – closer to the moment
I've been dreaming about – when I declare my love
to you and you declare it back and we forget there's
anyone else around and – sister Annabel's in a coughing
fit yet again.

(Sigh.) It could never work. What would everyone say?
What would I even say? Not that it would matter. You'd
simply rest your hand on my shoulder, whilst placing a
finger to my lips and your eyes would lock with mine...
listen to me, I'm a mess! If anyone found out what I was
thinking, I'd be thrown out for sure. But is it a sin to fall
in love? Sure it would be a scandal – you're probably
two...maybe even three times my age – but we could
leave, build a new parish together somewhere.

As the offering plate finishes making its rounds, the
service is drawing to a close. Something in me says

it's now or never. My heart is thumping...what do I do?
That's it! I grab a pen and a hymn sheet...ah I can't
think...*(scribbles)* '*I would part the Red Sea for you.*' No
that's awful. '*Let's be like Noah and do this as a pair.*'
Gosh that's somehow worse. '*I know you've already
given your heart to Jesus, but is there more space for
me?*' ... I think that's about as good as it'll get. Right here
it goes, deep breath. With the grace of an elephant on
three legs I attempt to stealthily walk past your pew
and slide you the hymn sheet. Oh no, you've passed
it on! Why did you pass it on? Oh goodness, Barry's
got it now. Please don't see the message, please don't
see the message! Crap he's reading it...he's smiling at
me. Oh this is bad. Please stop smiling. Why won't he
stop smiling? Oh gosh, he's making love hearts with his
hands now. I think I might faint. That's when I feel it –
your gentle hand touching my arm. I knew it! This love is
real. To hell with caution, I grab your hand and declare –
'I love you! I love you and I don't care who knows.'

The place falls silent. Barry looks heartbroken.
Sheepishly you tell me you just wanted a hymn sheet.
It all comes crashing down! The entire congregation has
witnessed the whole thing. I've got nothing left to lose,
I might as well at least make my case,

'You know Father when I joined the nunnery, I was
nothing more than an innocent girl. My world was simple
and my biggest issue was figuring out how I could cycle
to church whist maintaining a modest skirt length – a
difficult task I'm sure my sister's will agree. Then I met
you. You complicated everything. Though we will never

know what could've been, know that you'll always have my heart. Thank you...for everything.'

I finally let go of your hand and make my way through the church as I unfasten my veil. Despite the awkward lingering silence, I walk through with my head held high. I came to the nunnery a girl, but now I leave having learned to love – a woman. Just as I reach the door, I remember one last thing,

'And Barry, you're a married man. Control yourself for goodness sake!'

A Long Time Coming

Hassan Abdulrazzak

> **A young man whose life as a producer becomes unravelled when the industry suspects that he is gay. For ages 18 and above.**

Stephen is in an apartment in Brooklyn, New York City. He is on the phone. Beep of answering message.

Pick up, Ricky! Pick up. This is Stephen. Some fucked up shit went down tonight. There's blood all over my clothes. Pick up, man. Shit!

OK, one way or another you're gonna hear this. Even if I have to spill my guts to your fucking answerphone, you're gonna hear it. We launched the album tonight. The club was packed! Everyone was there. MTV, UFX, VH1. Everybody. We kick off with 'Grab her by the pussy' and the crowd goes insane. That hook, man, what did I tell you? I was king of the world, tonight. Then Stacy, my little sister she cuts through the crowd. I didn't even know she was gonna be there.

'Why your lyrics be beating up on women, Stevie?'

Man that just cut right through me. The look in her eyes said you can hide from the world but you can't hide from me. Now I hear my lyrics again. But they sound different. They sound poison. 'Grab her by pussy. Grab her by the pussy'. The whole crowd is chanting it out loud.

37

I had to get away from her, Ricky. From her judging eyes. So I go upstairs, to the VIP lounge. Boosie leaps out of nowhere. Grabs me by the neck. And that's when shit got real.

Beep of answering message. Dials again.

Damn! What the fuck man, why aren't you answering? What time is it in London anyways? Shoot. It's 6am? No wonder you ain't answering.

Beat.

So Boosie, he takes me to a room in the back of the VIP. The guys are all there: Charlie, Tyrone, Li'l Shoe. And in the corner, dancing by herself is this blond. Boosie tells me 'She's for you. A gift for my main man, Stephen, who hit it outta the park tonight. You can tap that ass right here, right now.' So I say 'I ain't into hoes, you feel me?' But he says, she's no hoe. She's April from American Idol. She won the last season. She's been dying to meet me. April scoots over, eyes all glazed, and starts dancing with me without asking. She turns around and now her ass is rubbing against my cock. The guys are hooting and screaming 'Tap that ass, tap that ass.'

Boosie is screaming at me. 'Grab her titties. Go on Stephen grab them big Southern corn-fed titties. They're yours. You earned them.' I can see April is too drunk or high or both to even know what's happening. I feel kinda sorry for her. I try to leave but Boosie pushes me back towards April. 'Do what your song says. Grab her by the pussy. Do it. Be a man.' And that's when I pick up the champagne bottle and crash! I bring it right on his head. Li'l Shoe screams 'Jesus, holy mother of crap!' I look at Boosie and I see blood pouring down his face. But that's not what scares me. What scares me is what he says next. 'I always knew you were a little faggot.'

I run out of there, Ricky as fast as I could. I didn't take the limo. I didn't call an Uber. I didn't even take the subway. I couldn't go home. Not after that. I ran all the way here. To your apartment. It's the only place I can be right now 'cause no one knows about it.

Damn! Why you not answering? I need you to answer. You're the only one I can talk to about this. You ashamed 'cause of the album? Is that it? You on my little sister's side now?

Now everyone expects me to be honest all of a sudden, lose the fan base I spent years building. Well, I ain't doing it. You hear me.

What will it take for you to pick up? You want me to say it? I don't want to say it to your answering machine you asshole. Alright. If that's what it takes.

If I say it, will you pick up? If I say what you've been wanting me to say all along, will you finally press accept? Alright. Alright.

I love you Ricky. Now please for the love of God's almighty cock, pick up.

A Man Of Hidden Talents

Edward Sayeed

A woman working in a charity shop is the object of her colleagues' affections. For ages 18 and above.

I mean, the thing is, I know Terrance means well. But he can't be doing that. End of the day, I am his boss. And if I'm lying there awake at night wondering how I can make the shop run better, then he can bloody do what he's meant to when he's working here. People ask me don't you get lonely since you and Ollie divorced, but I don't get lonely, I'm too busy to get lonely. What I do get is fed up when people who are given a job to do, don't do it.

Like this last time. The trousers were only three quid to begin with. Really nice corduroys from M&S. No tears or nothing. Three quid is not a lot to ask for them. If you go down Oxfam, by the bus stop, you'd be paying fifteen, I'm not joking, fifteen, *twenty* quid for them! Of course *Sue Ryder,* people think we're just cheap stuff. Only cos I don't pretend I'm running Harvey Nicks. I like to keep the prices down so the people who find the high street a bit dear can still afford to come here. But what I don't need, is that clumsy git Terrance taking pity on customers and putting the price down *again.* I've written three quid on those trousers, and what does he go and do? Offers them for a pound. One pound. I've come in from making a tea out back, and I've seen the customer fumble round in his pocket and give Terrance the pound and walk out looking pleased as anything. Gave Terrance an extra large thank you as well. You know like *'Thanks mate'*, like he knew he'd got a deal. And Terrance kinda gave me a sly look, and sort of turned away to look out the window and I've gone 'Terrance, those trousers were supposed to be three pounds', and he's gone 'Were they?' And I can't take this anymore, I said 'Terrance, what's the matter with you? We priced 'em together this morning'. And he turns to me with his sad, hurt little face, on his big bear's body and he says, 'The bloke looked like maybe he didn't have three quid.' And I want to hug him and punch him at the same time, and I just say 'Terrance, if it says three pound, charge 'em three pound. Please!'

The next day he's off sick. And the day after that. And then all of the next week too. I mean there's sensitive and then there's just being silly. I've had Jill the sixth former helping, if you can call it helping. It's something she has to do to get credits at college. She doesn't know where things go and the way I like my tea and how we mark the prices in red for women's clothes and green for the men's and... Terrance is right out of order doing this. So I go round his house, knock on the door. No answer. I can hear someone in the hall though. He must have come and looked through the peep hole. So I call out, cos I know he can hear me, 'Terrance, you bloody idiot. You get back in the shop tomorrow.' Still no answer, so I've leant down to the letterbox to have another go at him, thinking to say something all mean but it's come out as, 'Terrance, I miss you, love.'

Pause.

Next morning, there he is, bright and early. Cheery, making me a tea, sorting the rails. He's got a nice blue cardy on, one I've not seen before and I'm thinking 'Ooo, someone's in a good mood'.

And then he lets a suit, a *suit*, go for two pound twenty. Lets the guy bargain him down from twelve quid, 'til the customer sees he can have it for nothing if he wants and ends up giving Terrance a couple of quid just to be polite. Does it in full view of me. And he's watching me, waiting for me to come and give him an earful...only I don't.

Few days later he's come in with new shoes. New. Not newish. Not charity shop new. New. He starts shaving. Everyday. And I could swear one day, he even had aftershave on. He certainly started wearing deodorant, which is a Godsend on hot days. And then he's asking me what films I like. Are there any I'd like to see that I haven't? Cheeky devil, as if I wanna go to the cinema with him. And I was wondering how to let him down gently, when I heard myself say, 'Yeah that new one set in space looks good', and he's whipped out a smartphone, right there and then and bought us a couple of tickets. Who'd have thought he knew how to work one of them. A man of hidden talents perhaps.

We shall see.

A Mountain to Climb

Yasmeen Khan

> **A young woman is one of the top servers selling cheese in a department store but is conflicted about an opportunity to intern for a record company. Age stated in monologue as 18 years old.**

MAYA, 18, is standing by a large food counter in a shop.

(To unseen woman a few feet away.) Emily? Emily...? Can I just / Could we have a chat a bit later? Just so...Oh...I /

That's two days I've tried now. I think she's avoiding me, you know. She's so wrapped up in this big event she's planning, but I just need, like, five minutes. I have to reply to an email today – a really important one – otherwise they're going to give it to someone else. Wait, she's coming back – *(To unseen Emily.)* Emily, please – oh she's got a customer with her.

She had way more than five minutes for me when I came for my interview – kept saying I was just what they were looking for. I was well happy, I'd been looking for work for months. But be careful what you wish for, right, because I was desperate, I wanted a job, any job, and I ended up here. I never thought they'd put me in this department. Of course I couldn't tell her that I'm... Well I couldn't say it, because I really need money. And then

43

when I saw which counter I was going to be put on –
I just thought that was it, game over, but...turns out I'm
good at it. Who would have known that – that I – me
– am top salesperson in Harrod's cheese department.
Cheese mountain, they call this. It's not even a dairy
department, just cheese. Every type of cheese you can
imagine. One hundred and seventy six different cheeses!
I didn't even know that many cheeses existed. I mean,
Dairylea, cheddar and Philadelphia was about my limit.
Oh no wait, those three, plus the 'light' versions of each.
So I've gone from six to a hundred and seventy six. Some
people might be excited by that, but... And all this blue
cheese... I mean, what is that...rich people pay a lot for
food that has technically gone off. But the thing that
Emily doesn't know, right, the thing I haven't told her,
is that...hold on –

(To unseen customer.) Hello madam, would you like to
sample anything today from our cheese mountain? We
have this West Country organic goats cheese just in,
so creamy, have a taste? *(Pause.)* Oh, yeah, I'm lucky, I
can eat it all the time madam! Had it for lunch just now.
(Pause.) A hundred grams? Tell you what, how about
two hundred and fifty, it works out cheaper? *(Pause.)*
Perfect! I'll pack that up for you and you can get it on
your way out. Thanks! Bye!

Emily reckons I could sell cheese to a dairy farmer. Says
I could really go far here. I'm like...yeah...right to the top
of cheese mountain. But what Emily hasn't sussed out is
that I...am lactose intolerant. I can't eat any of this. Oh,
I have a tiny bit in front of her and give it all the mmmm,
yeah, yum-yum, but it's stressful pretending! And I don't

want her to get rid of me – because there's probably some health and safety rule that would mean she'd have to, right? So I'm nodding and smiling when Emily's excited about some new Gouda, but... I don't want to do this. See, I've got this internship, at a big record company. I can't believe it. Look I'm not stupid, right, it's an unpaid internship, I know I'm just going to be making tea and doing filing and all that, but...that's how it starts, right? The big opportunity you read all these big artists talking about. They've emailed me twice now. They said if I don't get back to them by the end of today they'll have to give to someone else. If I could just get the chance to get to show them my stuff.

Emily caught me beatboxing once. She thought I was choking. Tried to give me that what do you call it, Heimlich manoeuvre thing! Security come running over, a woman starts screaming, it all kicked off. And when I explained, poor Emily, she didn't know what to say. Turns out she's on some medication for her nerves. Been through a bad time, I don't know what, though. Said anything unusual makes her jumpy. I guess if you found a member of staff making a weird noise by the camembert, you'd call an ambulance as well. Poor Emily. Knowing her, she probably put herself on some cultural awareness course afterwards.

If I got the chance...if I could go a bit further with it, if I could get someone at the record company to actually hear me in person – because that's much better than sending them a link they're never going to click on, right? I've been on their internship waiting list for eight months. I just need Emily to let me go for three weeks. I'm not expecting her to pay me, but if she could keep my job open for me, maybe? But it's the same time as our annual Festival of Cheese – that's the big thing she's been busy planning. It's like a massive promotion, with press involved and loads of suppliers banking on it. It's a big deal for her.

Emily... she's... well she wears all nice expensive dresses with flowers on them. She's nice, really nice. Speaks nice, looks nice, acts...nice. It's not that I don't rate what she does, I know being in charge of Harrod's food hall is a big job. It's her life. She doesn't have kids or a boyfriend or anything, she literally lives here. *(Beat.)* It's not what I want. But I think she feels like she's rescuing me. Like, I'm her project, or something. To be fair she did give me a chance when nobody else would. *(Beat.)* Maybe I should just quit. Like if I'm going to go for it, I should just go for it, right? But...what if I'm...what if I can't do it? *(Beat.)* At least here Emily thinks I'm good at my job. *(Beat.)*

I read this interview once, with this brilliant hip hop artist and he talked about your destiny coming towards you, racing down the track like...like a runaway train? And how he always knew he would end up doing what he loved, like he didn't have a choice. I get that, you know, I get that. But what if that train is one you want to get out of the way of, to run, screaming in the opposite direction. But you can't. It's like you're being pulled towards it like it's some huge magnet and it's not going to stop 'til you're on board. On the train all the way to the top of cheese mountain. *(Beat.)*

It's just an internship. I'll just be making tea for people who don't even notice I'm there, right? People who come here and pay a lot for food with mould in it. *(Beat.)* Maybe I'll just tell them thanks, but I can't make it. Maybe I could do it another time? Or, maybe... *(Beat. She gets her phone out, looks at it, hesitates, puts it back in her pocket.)*

(To unseen customer.) Would you like to try the new West Country goats cheese, madam?

A Sweet Life

Guleraana Mir

> **A short monologue about how easy a dog's life is, so why not be one? For ages 18 and above.**

Look. Calm down, OK? I'm right here. I'm a medical professional, remember that?

(Beat.) You're a medical professional for christ's sake, you've got this. I trust you. I do.

Otherwise I wouldn't have asked you to... My anaesthetic is about to kick in, and I need your hand to be steady. Can you do that for me? Find your zen place. Find it, settle in and then we'll get started.

Did I ever tell you about our Frank? Our labradoodle? He's the reason I started on this journey. He saved my life one Christmas. We were out, playing in the snow, completely freaked him out, but he loved it. So we're playing and I hear my mother scream 'Don't go onto the ice Kelly!'. I've ventured right on top of the edge of the frozen pond, and it's unstable, it's...of course the ice cracked.

(Beat.) And of course I fall in. Frank saves me. He jumps straight in, no thought for his own safety. But then I suppose he wouldn't would he? He wouldn't think, just do. That's a dog's prerogative.

And that's when I started thinking about it.

REALLY thinking about a dog's life. What do they do? They learn a couple of tricks, big deal. Lie down, roll over, I'd do that if someone was going to feed me treats. And belly rubs, how intimate are they? You like belly rubs, don't you? Who doesn't? It's a sweet life if you ask me. You know dogs do the same thing over and over again and no one bats an eyelid. For humans, that's the very definition of insanity, but dogs...

So that's when I became a human puppy. I had an outfit made that looks just like Frank, and when I put it on I feel closer to him.

Everything becomes so much more simple, you know? When I'm running free in the park, it feels like a time out from the stress of the infinite loop of boob jobs, nose jobs, tummy tuck. It's not irresponsible, it's respite, getting back to my carnal self. And just as I thought life couldn't get better I realised it's not real, is it? It might be authentic, but it's not real. That's when I decided I could do this...make medical history.

Oh. I can't feel my arse, that means it's time. Are you ready to change the world? Go on, get your gloves on and grab the tail from the fridge. *(Beat.)* I can't believe we're doing this, Frank would be so proud!

A Thousand Hours
Mina Barber

> **A girl has a place on a singing competition
> and has dreams of being the first girl in a hijab
> to win. If only she can sing Morrissey and not
> Whitney. For ages 16 to 21.**

SELINA's bedroom.

*Depeche Mode's 'Personal Jesus' plays, SELINA dances
and sings along as if no one is watching, as if she's at her
own personal concert.*

*It's as if the song then transfers to her headphones
and the lights come up to her bedroom. Suddenly she
doesn't look cool anymore but awkward.*

'Reach out and touch faith, Your own personal Jesus,
Someone to hear your prayers, Someone who cares'

> *She suddenly stops and turns the music off.*

How long have you been there? Yeah I know this is your
room too, yeah alright technically a hotel so it's not
anyone's, you're soooo clever Shefali. When did you get
back? Mum's at work.

Just stay on your side of the room yeah, that's what the
cardigan line is for. No, I don't wanna share a room with
my stupid sister either. You think we're gonna get out of
here? Whatever, that's just noise from the housing.

What, what was I doing? None of your business.

I was practising, OK? It's the final round tomorrow.

> *She puts her headphones in and starts to sing/speak the words of Whitney Houston's 'One Moment In Time' as if she's learning the song. Her heart isn't in it.*

'Each day I live, I want to be, a day to give, the best of me'

Blah, blah, blah

'I want one moment in time, when I'm more than I thought I could be'

Nothing's wrong...what face? I'm not pullin' a face. Yeah, yeah of course I wanna sing. You don't understand... it's like... I'm leaving my body when I sing. You're gonna say it's 'Haram' but when I sing it's like I've got a private audience with Allah. Shut up, I'm not high.

They said if I do Whitney I'm guaranteed a place in the final round. I'd be at the judge's houses, but, like you don't touch Whitney, I mean Whitney's Whitney.

Shef, please, please just let me say it yeah... I wanna sing my songs! I wanna dress in black and wear black eyeliner. I mean I might leave the white face powder, yeah, I don't wanna look like a 'bhoot'* – like Casper the Friendly Ghost. Like that Jusnara at school, her mum reckons she'll get a better husband if she puts on the white powder. Stupid innit? But like Shefali, I wanna listen to The Cure day and night? I wanna write beautiful and sad lyrics, you know that you have to listen to over and over again to get the meaning, like Sylvia Plath.

What do you mean? Yeah I'm sure there are Bengali goths, why not?! Then I'll be the first!

Shef you gotta see their faces – the first girl in a hijab on British TV in a big singing competition. They asked all these stupid questions like, 'Do you live on a council estate?', 'Have you ever lived on a council estate?' They really want me to live on a council estate? And I said I did, well kind of...and they carried on, 'Is there anyone disabled in your family?', 'Do you claim benefits?' Like they would give us extra points if we said 'Yes'. Then they were like, 'Have you had any personal tragedies?' Something really heart-wrenching they said. I told them about Dad dying, but they said that was years ago. They wanted something more recent... I wish I hadn't now, but I told them about the fire in the block and guess what they said, 'Which one?'... Yeah, but when is that money gonna come through? We haven't heard nothin' from the council! They keep sayin' any day now, but when is that? How many more days? How many more hours? A thousand! Because we've already done that! I'm not talking nonsense! Yes alright, I am not angry, OK.

They're gonna come round on Wednesday and do some filming for the show. Yes, here! They wanna do a whole 'Strong and Stable' piece they said...but, I don't feel strong, I just wanna... I'm sorry. Yeah, takeaway, what else?

... I know 'FAKE IT UNTIL YOU MAKE IT'...

It's as if her sister has left. Selina turns on her headphones again she sings the first few lines of 'One Moment In Time' her voice cracks as she fights to hold back tears.

'Each day I live, I want to be, a day to give, the best of me'

She changes the song.

'A Thousand Hours' by The Cure plays out.

She smiles at first then screams into her hands and cries as she listens to the song lyrics.

bhoot – Ghost

Ace of Clubs

Rachel Coombe

A doctor meets her childhood bully. For ages 25 and above.

When I was ten years old, an older girl at school punched me in the face and broke my nose. I remember being absolutely stunned, furious, and confused. What did I do to her? I tried to think back and remember if we'd ever had an argument, but I came up blank. The school called my dad, who came with me to A&E. We sat in silence in the waiting room. He took a pack of playing cards from his pocket and handed them to me. I was in agony, with my head tilted right back and tissues stuffed up my nose, but the feel of the cards between my fingers as I cut the pack again and again soothed me, and made the pain fade into the background. I had shuffled them at least twice when I realised the Ace of Clubs was missing from the pack.

Yesterday at work, I'd just finished my break when I was told my next appointment had arrived. I immediately recognised my patient. She hadn't changed much at all. She was still solid, chunky, and her face devoid of expression apart from a slight sneer at the right corner of her fleshy mouth.

I still remembered the look on her face as she slammed her fist into my nose all those years ago. She didn't seem to recognise me. I felt my shoulders tense and my breathing become shallow. Damn panic attacks. They'd been mild at first and barely noticeable, but now they were the bane of my life. They slightest thing could set them off.

I looked at her card and tried to control my breathing, focusing on the feeling of the card in my hand. Kari Brennan. Nose breaker extraordinaire.

Hello, Kari, I'm Doctor Jhun. Take a seat and I'll check your eyes.

This was the first time in my career I had to give a patient such awful news. Two weeks after the incident, I joined a local kids' magic club. I practised every chance I got. I made friends with other 'magic' kids.

Pick a card, Kari, any card.

Kari pressed her forehead against the machine and I checked her eyes, slowly, the whole time hoping that I'd made a mistake and that I would send her out into the bright, sunny day with good news.

Don't let me see me your card, keep it to yourself.

It was bad. Her eyesight in her left eye was declining so quickly I was surprised she didn't seem more worried, but maybe she was just in denial, or she thought it was temporary.

Remember your card, Kari. Now put it back into the pack.

Her right eye wasn't looking so great, either. She was going to need surgery in the next few days if she was going to keep her sight in that eye. I could feel a panic attack coming on as I realised that I was going to have to give her news that was going to change her life.

I shuffled the cards. I remember my dad always used to say 'Let's do this, Kiddo.'

Let's DO this.

I put my hands on either side of Kari's face, my thumbs on her eyelids. She pulled away from me, horrified.

It's OK, Kari, it's going to be OK.

I could feel my hands start to vibrate; the layers of glazed film start to retract from over her right cornea, her eye muscles start to tighten, the blur of her fading vision starting to disappear.

Is this the card you chose, Kari of course it is.

Ace of clubs, I thought. You picked the Ace Of Clubs.

Acting Up

Edward Sayeed

> The influence a teacher has over a boy who
> loves acting. For school ages.

D'you know what it is? It's like, you're more yourself
when you're not being yourself. I know that sounds
funny, but when I'm *me*...it's like I'm trapped... When I'm
being a character, I'm alive. That's why, when I heard
about method acting, I was like, that's me. That's what
I've been doing. I never had a name for it. I never knew
it was some theory that was made up in New York or
before that in Russia, but that's what I've always done.
Everyday at school, I'd do a different character. One day
I'd be a kid who'd been adopted by travellers cos there'd
been some who lived near us so I'd seen what they
were like. I'd act tough and quiet, and if anyone said
something to me, I'd answer like *(strong Irish accent)*
'Alright. Yeah, I'm fine.' Another day I'd be American,
Scottish, mix it up. But always, the one I choose in the
morning, stick with it the whole day.

It really started when I was in Mrs Wright's class. She'd
just had a baby. Showed us photos. Little Freddie. And
she was *tired*. She give me five minutes at the start of
each lesson to do my thing in front of the class. It was
just a bit of fun for me, but she told me at the end of
school one day what it meant for her, getting that time
off. How it helped her and Freddie. And she'd always

tell my mum how I was doing well. Alright, I weren't too strong on science, and Mum'd got some idea I was gonna be a doctor, but other than that, things were good.

The next year I had Mr Matthews... *(Whistles.)* First day after summer holidays I'm acting as Clint Eastwood in *The Good, The Bad and The Ugly*. You know where they ask him a question and he's like... *(Pause. Breathy voice:)* 'Yeah.' Just like a really long pause and one word answer. And I can see Mr Matthews thinking, 'What's the matter with this boy?' But he never said nothing, until the next day I come in as a kid from Yorkshire who's got ADHD. I hadn't quite got the Yorkshire accent down, but the ADHD, my cousin's got it, so that was easy. He'd make us sit down, I'd get up. He'd ask someone else a question, I'd answer it, even if what I said was nothing to do with what he asked. I could see him getting stressed, and I'm not lying now, I felt bad about that, I never wanted to piss him off, but... I dunno why, but I've had this feeling, since I started doing my acting, or acting up like Mr Matthews called it, that it was something I *had* to do. I dunno why.

Mr Matthews spent a year, ignoring everything I said and did. He got all the other kids laughing at me. Always going, 'Oh Jake's being stupid today as usual'. And though he never spoke to me, he talked to Mum. Makes a special point of telling her how I'm getting behind in science. Then this one Friday afternoon I'm playing an MI5 agent. I'm writing out all the notes, careful, like so no one can look over my shoulder, saying things in a code that I only I know. And I can see this look, like hatred, like pure hatred in Mr Matthews' eyes. And I just know he's gonna be calling up Mum and having some mean conversation with her tonight. So cos I can't be dealing with Mum right after she's been speaking to Mr Matthews I walk a long route home, through the park, behind the shopping centre and I go down this road I've never been down before and I see this building...it's a drama...school... *You can get a school for drama?* And I'm like, I've found the place for me! I run home quick, gonna tell Mum, and it's all gonna be good now. Course she's just got off the phone from Mr Matthews so when I talk about drama school she's like, 'You joking, that ain't happening.'

Next week in school, I'm sitting in the playground at lunchtime. Just me. Don't wanna talk to none of the other kids, they're always taking the piss. Mrs Wright comes up to me. She could see I weren't too good. She asks me what's up and I tell her. She don't say much, goes back to the staffroom. But when I get home that night, Mum's all different, all like, 'Seeing how you're already doing acting anyway, maybe you should go have a look at that drama school'. Mum'd wanted me to be a doctor so I could help people. But Mrs Wright's called her and said that I'd helped someone already with my acting. Little kid called Freddie.

I ain't gonna lie. When I started at the drama college, I couldn't help seeing that there weren't many...well it was mainly, like white kids...and like quite a lot of them's quite posh. But fuck it. Acting's in my blood. I had to come here. And there were enough people here that got what I was about, let me run with it.

EDWARD SAYEED

I got my stage debut tomorrow. Playing a Canadian priest. It's been hard, staying in one character for six weeks.

I've got Mrs Wright a ticket. Maybe I'll get one for Mr Matthews as well. I'll write a little letter with his ticket. I'll say, 'cos I know you always liked my acting'.

Assassin's Prayer

Olivia Furber

> **An assassin with a conscience is asking God for some help. For ages 21 and above.**

Dear Lord. I need you to...

No, it's not a request line.

Dear Lord. Firstly, thank you for the weather we are having. And for the sunset this evening. It was stunning. Sky was glowing as if the Messiah himself might show up.

That's just a phrase. Obviously, Jesus isn't coming back until the end of days when you command it. I know my Bible. Basically, I love it when you send a nice sunset to finish the day off. Praise be to you.

Right. Secondly, Lord... I need you to give me some advice. I know this isn't a call and response thing we've got going on here but if you could please, please show me a sign or reveal yourself to me, like you've done before. I would be eternally grateful.

I need your help. At work. I've got an assignment to do and I... I'm just having doubts, OK?

It started last night, as you know, because you are almighty and therefore see and hear everything. I was sleeping, and an ugly dream came to me. So dark and twisted it woke me up. And, as you know, my dreams are like prophecies.

They tell me when dark things have happened and I need to react. And then I got the call. A new assignment.

The voice on the end of the line was a woman's. Shaky and whispering half sentences through her tears. She's being abused by her husband in the worst kind of ways. Once she tried to retaliate and pushed him off of her and he smacked her in the face with a saucepan.

I took the job. How could I not? As we've discussed before, God, it's never about the money. It's about taking justice into my own hands and doing your work here on earth. These CRIMINALS are headed straight for Hell and I just make sure their ticket is first class.

But recently, I've been getting this gnawing, chewing feeling in my stomach when I work. It's doubt. I'm doubting myself, doubting you – I'm sorry, you know how that feels because St. Thomas did it to you. I need you to tell me where this feeling is coming from. Are you testing me? Am I still part of your plan? Or is this one of your more mysterious messages telling me that I need a career change?

I love my job and I love doing your work. But it's hard to switch off sometimes. Sounds replay in my head. The click of the trigger, the thud as a newly dead body hits the ground like a sack of potatoes. Sometimes I drive to Margate to hear the sound of the car's engine and the lapping of waves instead. Or I put in my headphones listen to 'Ave Maria'. Loud.

I know that life ends with a trial. No second chances. So I want to make sure that when we meet on the day of judgement that you're going to be giving me the keys to heaven's door. Not the other way round. Do you know what I mean?

Broken

Yasmeen Khan

> **A young boy heavily affected by his late uncle finds inspiration. Age stated in monologue as 21 years old.**

FEMI, 21, wearing a suit, is in his bedroom at home, practising a speech in the mirror.

'Everything has a solution. Everything can be built, everything broken can be mended.' *(He looks at the paper his speech is written on.)*

Do I sound alright, Uncle Femi? *(Beat.)* Apparently if you pretend everyone is naked, then you're less nervous. But the thought of it is making me more nervous!

> *He puts the speech in his pocket and pulls a Rubik's Cube out.*

This was the first thing you taught me. I remember you said if I do a Rubik's cube, I'd understand logic. You were right, you know. You'd be surprised how knowing that everything can be fixed has helped me – especially down at B&Q – I've been employee of the month three months running, did I tell you that? Even this month, when everything got...really tough. Guess I just threw myself into it. *(Beat, suddenly more upbeat.)* If you work in a DIY place, everything is either already broken, or the customer needs to fix something broken, or the process of actually doing DIY has...broken them. Sometimes I pull out the cube...the older customers laugh cos they haven't seen one for ages. Once you've got someone to laugh, all the stress, all the broken-ness, it's a lot easier to deal with. You taught me that too. *(Beat.)* Guess I've got a lot to thank you for, right?

He looks back into the mirror and tries his speech again.

'Everything has a solution. Everything can be built, everything broken can be mended.' *(Beat.)* I sound lame.

He moves away from the mirror.

Do you remember when you first realised that I liked making and fixing things? It was a long time before Mum and Dad did. I always preferred being in my bedroom, reading, learning, exploring – Mum and Dad said it was because I wanted to be away from people. Like that was a bad thing. But you were the one that turned that round, you saw it differently – you were the one who said it was because I wanted to make things. And you know that first model kit you bought me? I've still got it.

He pulls out a less than perfectly constructed model airplane from under the bed.

Yeah, I know, not my best work! *(Beat.)* But you said it was perfect. *(Beat.)* You must have spent so much money on all those models over the years. I never even thought about that until now...sorry. Mum said I was shaming her, taking all that stuff off you, but I was just so excited that I could make them sometimes without even needing to look at the instructions. And I never had any pieces left over! I should work in Ikea not B&Q! *(Beat.)* Hold on, Mum's shouting for me.

Responding to a voice from offstage.

Yeah I know, Mum, I'm coming! This is important! Two minutes! *(Beat.)*

Look, Uncle Femi, before it all starts getting really busy today and before...well, before everything that has to happen, I just wanted you to know – I'm glad you ignored what Mum said about the model kits making me spend more time on my own. Cos I wasn't on my own was I, I was with you. Mum says I'm obsessed with fixing stuff. Like that's a bad thing. She says I need to stop and that I can't fix everything. Well she's wrong. *(He picks up the model airplane and frantically begins to fix it. After a few moments struggling, he slumps to a stop.)*

As soon as I get my exam results and leave B&Q, I want to go into medical research. Yeah, I know it's not engineering like we talked about, but... I really want to do it and it would just feel right, somehow. I've been reading a lot about it. One of our regular customers, Dr Phillips, he says he might be able to help me – he's doing up his whole house so he's been coming in a lot and we got talking. He works for one of these big research labs and he was telling me how brilliant it is when they make a breakthrough. A step closer to finding a cure. A step closer to fixing things. *(Beat.)*

Responding to a voice from offstage.

OK Mum, I just need one more practise then I'm coming.

He takes the speech out of his pocket, looks at it before putting it back in his pocket and stepping up to the mirror to address it, as if addressing an audience.

'Everything has a solution. Everything can be built, everything broken can be mended.' It was my Uncle Femi who taught me that. *(Beat, he begins to cry.)* But he was wrong, because nobody could fix him. My uncle, who I'm named after, well the last time I saw him, he asked me if I would speak today. It's the last thing he asked of me. In fact it's the only thing he ever asked of me. And when I said yes, he smiled and said 'Let's do the cube again.' *(He pulls out the Rubik's Cube.)* So I pulled it out of my pocket and he was still smiling as I started doing it. And when I looked up from the cube at him again, he'd... *(Beat. He stares at the cube before slowly putting it back in his pocket.)*

(To offstage.) I'm coming now, Mum. It's time. *(Beat.)* It's time.

Chanel

Mina Barber

> **A woman is giving an account of her abusive boyfriend, but she needs to decide how to go about it. For ages 18 and above.**

A room.

Yeah and what, it's just a bruise? Are you recording this? I don't trust no police, turn it off yeah. I said turn it off!

Look right I been in this room for time now, just, just tell me he's OK. Wait, you don't believe me do you? What? No I don't wanna report him. Oh just fuck off! I know what you're thinking? 'It's Chanel, that big-mouthed bitch with her hoop earrings, yeah, she deserves it' and maybe I do?

I just, I just didn't want him to hurt my little girl. She's little and he's not her dad and he said he was gonna hurt her. You don't know what he was like. Once yeah, we were in a restaurant and he pushed my face into the food...he wanted to teach me a lesson for answering back.

He used to push his fingers into my eye socket and then he used...he said I deserved it, and maybe I did? I know it's my fault; I made him jealous, I wanted to, for him to be jealous. The first time he hit me was at a party, and it was like a reflex, I mean I hit him back. I'm so tough aren't I?... I'm not tough OK, I let my boyfriend hurt me and guess what, I STILL WANT HIM, but it's all twisted up in my head and then he came, he came at me, and the, the knife went in and the blood it just started spreading and he, he was lying on the kitchen floor, and I just ran with my little girl and I'm shitting myself, because I'm gonna lose him, and I can't lose him, because I'm not, I can't work, without him. Just tell me what hospital he's been taken to?

What? Twenty minutes ago.

> *She becomes very distraught and cannot hold back the tears.*

No. No, no, no! That's not true, no, please I wasn't there with him, please, please, no it ain't true!

> *CHANEL sinks into a flood of tears and anguish.*

> *Suddenly the tears stop and she looks at the audience, her voice and entire demeanour changes. CHANEL is now a well-educated woman, she's still from the estate but she isn't the stereotyped estate girl.*

Bit too much?

> *She gets up and mutters as if she is rewinding the scene to herself and falls on the floor mechanically. She gets to a repeated point in her speech.*

'NO IT AIN'T TRUE!'... Damn this double negative, I know, I know it's a great indicator of informal speech, but I just can't do it...it's just a step too far, I mean, such poor grammar. Although, I mean, who are they more likely to believe? Chanel trashy estate girl who killed her violent boyfriend in self-defence, because that wouldn't be classed as murder, I mean self-defence, manslaughter really, two to ten years. Will it be worth it? I must say, the knife piercing through his cheating skin was pretty thrilling... I mean sometimes a double negative can resolve to a positive, right?

She takes some hoop earrings out of her pocket.

Hoop earrings? Or not? Or maybe just a scraped back ponytail?

She puts on the hoop earrings

Sometimes you have to play the game.

Ya get me?

Child of God

Ayesha Manazir Siddiqi

> **A young woman sets off to London with her Pink Floyd records, hoping to find her father. Age stated in monologue as 24 years old.**

SOPHIE, 24, has a phone or laptop, on which she adjusts the camera, checking her hair and make-up, before pressing record.

Hi. It's me. You're not picking up FaceTime so I'm sending this. I know you're annoyed I brought the records with me to London, and I just want to explain, OK? OK.

So, it's the band. The band's not just a hobby anymore. It's getting serious. We play two gigs a week, near where I live and, it's doing OK. Only beginning, but beginning. I play bass, back-up vocals sometimes...a bit of tambourine. Anyway, these records – the Pink Floyd, late Beatles and things, they're like the music we play! We play kind of like psychedelic rock slash folk, hard to explain but, I mean, so alike, Mum, what are the chances? So I couldn't leave them behind, you know?

I know you don't get it. 'Little Sophie, gone to London, doing heaven knows what'. But I'm happy here, I don't need a 'safety net' and all that. When you're doing what you love, none of that matters. What would I have done back in Buckworth? Gone to the pub on a Friday, cleaned the house on Saturday, church on Sunday, and then repeat and die? That's not me, Mum. I mean, just the way people looked at me down there. Remember at school, when Stacey said she wouldn't hold my hand 'cause she might turn brown? Ignorant. And you said, I remember, you said, 'Never you mind Sophie. You are a child of God.' You're always there. I know. But it's not nice to have to deal with things like that. No.

(*Examines her face in the camera.*) Remember, Mum, that story you told me. How, when I was born, my eyes were blue, blue like the sky? And then they slowly turned darker over three weeks. First green, then navy, then brown, and then black. Black like now. Black like his.

Why don't you ever tell me about him? All I know is that he left when I was in your tummy, and that you pray for his soul every Sunday. Pray for his soul! Ha. I would've left too if I were him. What was he meant to do there, with just cows, and a Tesco? He was probably used to opera and airplanes and fancy bars and things...yeah. Yeah. I wouldn't have stayed either.

He's probably right here. In London. And if there's ever, like, a Pink Floyd tribute or anything. I go. Just in case, you know? *I know* I don't know what he looks like. But it's OK. We'll just know, you know? He'll look at me and he'll see his eyes, his nose, his fingernails, his skin. He's the one that made my eyes black, you know? He breathed them into me, even after I was born. And he'll see me and he'll say, 'Sophie. I knew you'd like this kind of music. That's why I left the records behind. That's why I come to this place, waiting for you. And here you are. Come'

It sounds stupid to you, I know. But you don't get it, Mum. Something like that could happen to me. 'Cause don't forget, I'm a child of God.

Choices

Ayesha Manazir Siddiqi

> **A young man tries to find solace with his boyfriend's family after his mother refuses to accept his sexuality. Age stated in monologues as 25 years old.**

Have you ever really really wanted something, but then also wanted the opposite thing?

Like, you really, really want ice cream, but also to lose five pounds?

Or, like, a PS2 *and* new trainers? A beard...and a shave?

Usually I guess you just kinda pick one, get on with it. But sometimes, you get stuck. Like, with Joshua.

I met him at uni. In the library. He was. Ah. Just. Beautiful. The hair. That neck. Those shoulders. Ah. Just. Trust me. Beautiful. So beautiful.

And Joshua, he'd come out to his parents when he was eleven! And you know what they did? They bought him a cake! And they said to him, 'Son, we love you just the same. If not more.' I fuck you not. *If not more.*

He told me, to be twenty-five and still not out. That's like, 'a life of secrecy and shame'.

I told him it's not the same. My mum, you know, she's from the Caribbean...

He looked at me then, like (*scrutinizing*) 'Ohh, that explains it'.

I said, 'explains what,' and he went like, 'well, the way you look, you know, I thought – maybe Indian? Arabic? something like that.' I said why didn't you just ask and he said mate, it's 2017, nobody cares. He meant it in a good way, I guess. He said, 'James, she's your mum. She'll love you the same no matter what. And so will I.'

Ahhh, that's what he said. 'And so will I.' That's pretty much like saying, 'I love you,' right? But not quite, so I couldn't say it back, but I went like, 'Ah. Me too.'

So yeah, spoiler alert. Mum didn't say, 'love you the same, if not more'. She went like, 'no you're not.' Just that. 'No you're not.' 'I'm sorry, Mum,' I started fucking apologising like that. Then she said, cold as ice, 'listen James, you're either *that*, or you're my son. You decide.'

So I left. I went to Joshua and his mum's. Being with Joshua was like being in the womb. His mum had a big dinner to celebrate, invited all her friends over. She said to them, 'This is James. Joshua's boyfriend,' that was nice, she called me his boyfriend. But then she said, 'Poor boy, his mum chucked him out'. And they all went like, tsk tsk, well, you're safe now. And yeah...the next morning at breakfast, she says to me, 'You know. If you were still in Africa, they'd have hung you for that.' That felt weird to me, when she said that. I told Josh. He just kind of said, 'I think she meant it in a good way.'

So yeah, I left Josh's too. And now, I sleep – well... I sleep where I can. And it's OK, it's bearable. Just, sometimes, when it gets cold or lonely, I close my eyes and I pretend. I pretend like I'm back in that warm, tiny bedroom at Mum's. Or, I pretend like I'm with Joshua.

Christie
NSR Khan

> A woman has an out-of-body experience as she deals with a client. For ages 18 and above.

Did he just say that? 'What am I getting for £260 per hour?' Ugh!

His suit must be worth a couple of thou'. I'd say Armani, but I'd be wrong. It's classier than that, bespoke probably. His face is so red and sweaty that he looks dirty and cheap. His massive ring, jade and platinum, looks nasty on his short fat fingers. This shipping company guy. Today's client.

He's complaining. Some tiny, delay on an affidavit. I was up 'til three a.m. working on his case.

He's shouting so much, other people can hear. I can see them looking through the glass walls. I wish I'd drawn the blinds.

He knows I'm a trainee. He threatens complaints. He is basically one big menace.

Insists that I get the senior partner here.

'Now!'

I can actually smell his stink, under the aftershave. How is that even possible? Being so rich and having such bad B.O.?

But that's good, actually. I can use this. His B.O. I need to focus on that. If I keep on thinking: 'You are a short, fat smelly man. And £260 per hour plus V.A.T. does not earn you the right to bully me.' Then words will start to form. I'll be able to say something to stop him shouting. But he's winning. The shouting is louder, like a police siren. I can't concentrate. I'm losing focus. I am beginning to panic. Is my mouth even opening? This is bad. I touch my lucky charm. It's folded in my pocket. I keep it there always. Except that's embarrassing, calling it that. Isn't it? A lucky charm? But it's what reminds me of who I am. That I am...that I should be invincible.

When the article came out in the *Camden New Journal*, I photocopied it. Twenty-five copies. And put a copy in every bag and jacket that I own. 'Student from Pupil Referral Unit graduates from Cambridge with Double First and goes on to city law firm'. My lucky charm. That's me. That's who I am and it's THE TOP city law firm, actually.

And then it happens. Like it does every time when I think I have no control. This thing my brain has been doing, since I was very, very small. It sort of separates and suddenly I'm floating above the room. The room is a blur. I can't smell him anymore. I'm up here. I can still see him shouting his face off. But I can't hear him anymore.

It's called a maladaptive defence mechanism. A reaction to childhood trauma. A lack of integration of identity. An enemy to intimacy. Makes it difficult to keep friends. But friendship can be a little overrated. No? To me...well this thing that my mind does, well... I call it survival, actually.

I've been practicing. Converting this disassociation into something else. I've learnt how when my mind floats off, that I can imagine a different reality. So suddenly I see myself, down there in the room with him – and I've lent across the desk and slapped him right back in his seat. I'm telling him to 'settle down'. He looks very small. And I look elegant and powerful. I can smell my perfume and feel the crispness of my three-piece suit. It's from ASOS, actually. But on me it looks good. Me down there in my £90 suit. Me...she...yes...me... I am, at this moment, invincible.

And he's back on his side of the desk. He looks like he's been told off. Like he has settled down. I feel myself float back. I am literally 'back in the room'. The smell, the B.O., that's still there, but not so strong. I can hear him telling me, 'You're worth every penny of my £260.'

What a win! I just wish I could tell someone. Like a friend, maybe.

Dateception

Tessa Hart

> **An imam at a speed dating event reveals too much. For ages 18 and above.**

Hi. I'm Mohsin.

You look lovely.

Have you come from far today?

My journey was quite quick, I was listening to the radio. I really enjoy listening to the radio.

> *Tries to hide that he is cringing at his own words for a moment.*

So...nice weather today...

> *Cringes even more and pauses for a moment before continuing.*

Anyways, it's lovely to meet you...

> *Awkward pause.*

Only three minutes, eh, we better get to business! Ha! That's a lovely dress by the way I have one just like it.

I mean, ehm...

> *Awkward pause.*

TESSA HART

Yeah, yeah... I have a dress.

No, it's my dress.

I bought it.

Because I liked it.

Yeah, yeah, I have other dresses. I really like dresses.

I wear them.

I just enjoy dressing up. Dresses and other women's clothes.

Yes really.

Men's clothes are so monotone but women's fashion is so creative, and inspiring and diverse, I love getting into that. Literally!

I'm not gay; I just really enjoy wearing women's clothing.

Oh no, I don't do performances like that! It's unthinkable with my profession.

Oh, never mind.

No really, you don't need to know.

Look, it doesn't matter. Anyways, tell me more about yourself!

Oh, alright then, sit back down, please, I'll tell you...

Whispers.

I'm an imam.

Slightly louder, but still whispering.

An imam. I'm an imam!

Yes, really. I swear by Allah.

Not the most common profession, I suppose, but I love it. I knew it was what I wanted to do since I was quite young.

Yes, really. There's nothing that I'm as passionate about as the true teachings of the Quran and helping the members of my community...

Well except maybe one other thing that I'm nearly as passionate about...

There is a signal that time is up.

Are three minutes up already?

Look, I can't believe I told you this. Please don't tell anyone!

If the Mosque committee found out...

I'm sorry I've just kept on babbling on and now you barely had a chance to say anything.

Calling after her.

Where are you going? You'll tick my name, right?

Dear Mr President

Tessa Hart

> **A young woman tries to find a way to tell her
> father, who is a president, that she might not
> live up to all what is expected of her. For ages
> 18 and above.**

Hello... Mr President.

I mean... Sir.

Or well... Baba.

Hi Baba.

It's been a while, so I thought I'd give you a call.

Yes, I know it's been a year.

Yes, I do know how to use a phone...

Anyways, how are you?

And how's the country doing? Any major crises or
revolutions lately?

Uni? Erm...yeah uni's great.

No, I'm not just partying; I'm going to class!

Yes, Baba, I know you don't need another scandal on
your hands.

It's not my fault someone sold pictures of me to that shitty paper!

I know, I know, a decent girl wouldn't have been drunk and dressed like that in the first place; do you have to keep on going on about it?

Oh come on, pictures of me partying are hardly going to throw the country into crisis again; I'm not quite as impactful as the murder of an MP...

I did not look like a prostitute and even if I did, so what!

No, Baba, I'm not a prostitute and I'm still going to uni, OK?!

Trying to calm down again.

Actually...that's kind of why I'm calling...

No, not prostitution Baba, uni!

Look... Baba... You know how I was studying banking and finance?

Well... I switched to drama.

Drama.

Yes, drama.

Baba, I switched my course to fucking drama!

No, not *fucking* drama, just drama. Drama! How many times do I have to say it?

No, I'm not trying to create drama, I'm studying drama.

I mean, yes, so I'm kind of trying to create drama, but not in that sense.

No, I'm not studying to be a prostitute now, will you stop calling me a fucking prostitute, please.

Beat.

You know, I wasn't even going to tell you.

But I didn't want to not talk to you for three years because what if something happened to you in those three years and then I could never talk to you again.

And I know you have other things to worry about because you have a country to run and the next crisis to prevent and I don't want to cause any more trouble... again.

But I need to tell you the truth.

So I'm going to call, Baba.

I'm going to call.

She gets out her phone and looks at it.

I'm going to call.

She continues looking at the phone.

Discuss
Karim Khan

> A school teacher is interrupted by her class
> who have videos of her stealing from a
> supermarket. For ages 21 and above.

[-]: silent interjections from Miss Patel's class.

'The best things in life are free'. Discuss. So I want you
to use Gatsby *(brandishes novel)* to make a case for
why you think the best things in life are free or, why
you think the best things in life are not free – offering a
counterargument. And what I want you to do is to write
that essay through one of the characters in the novel,
choose whoever you want, but, but I want you to treat it
as an academic essay not a character monologue – I'm
expecting...the same level...of sophistication – uh, can
you quieten down please. I want you to hand it in to
me on Thursday the fourteenth...is something wrong?
(Walks forward).

What's funny?

Haven't I told you to stop going on your phones during
class. I'll confiscate it again. *(She looks around. Laughs
nervously.)*

Is this some kind of joke? You're all on your phones.
Why are you laughing? Here. Let me see please. *(She*

takes a phone and watches a video.)

Who filmed this? Who made this video? Oh.

She looks at the class, suddenly vulnerable.

Be quiet please. [-]

I did not steal cherries...from Sainsbury's! *(Pause.)*

Quiet down please. The video is completely wrong... I paid for them, you didn't film me paying for them. I use my handbag as a basket to carry my shopping you see. If I'm going to pay for my shopping anyway, it doesn't matter where I put it does it? Could you all delete it... immediately. [-]

Don't threaten me, you can't do that, that's wholly an immoral thing to do. [-]

I haven't done anything immoral – I did not steal anything. Let me show you the receipt – I probably have it here somewhere. *(Rummages through handbag.)* It must be somewhere. Bear with me please. I know it's here, where is it? I don't think it's here, must be at home or in my car. I'm not lying. I'm not a thief. I...sometimes...it doesn't matter,

No...you won't understand.

I sometimes have this compulsion to take things and, I don't, I don't want it, I don't need it. I just take it and go. But I always return the things the next day because I'm not a thief. I've got some problems that I need help with, and I'm getting...slowly, but I'm not a thief.

DJ Kibbles

Mr Ekow

> A quirky monologue about a wannabe DJ
> enlisting the help of a cat to get the party
> going. For ages 18 and above.

It's that time of year again: Pete won't make it past
eight, Sarah will be all over an unsuspecting intern
and one stupid, but courageous person will tell the
boss what everyone has wanted to all year: shove
your memos up your arse! You've gotta love an office
Christmas party. I certainly do. Because for at least two
hours I get to pretend my DJ career didn't end with
those uni raves. You see there's levels to this: go to most
office parties and no doubt someone will have stuck on
a playlist of Buble, Wham!, Mariah Carey – you know,
the usual suspects. Me? I'm talking two decks, a mic
and a whole lot of vinyl. Yeah I throw in a few Christmas
favourites, but you can't beat a bit of Oxide & Neutrino
to get the walls shaking. Highlight of the year I'd say. My
manager asked if I wanted to take a break this time with
everything that's gone on at home...but I can't leave my
adoring fans waiting can I?

Well anyway, every year I try to work in some sort of
gimmick – you know, do something crazy people will
remember. Well I just happened to stumble on the
perfect thing – a cat DJ. Yeah I know it sounds crazy,
but believe me Miss Kibbles can scratch! I used to hate

the bloody thing, but she's finally proving her worth.
Now how does a cat DJ I hear you ask? Well long story
short, the other day I'm clearing some stuff at the flat...
cos it had been awhile, since Rich had erm you know...
anyway I found his favourite vinyl – Ms Dynamite,
'Booo!'...we both loved that song growing up. Really he's
the one that got me into music in the first place when
I think about it... So I load it up onto my home setup
and immediately I'm reminiscing of fake IDs and pulsing
subs when all of a sudden Miss Kibbles jumps on to the
decks. The stupid thing's spinning in circles. I go to get
her off, but I kid you not – I start to hear some decent
scratches being made. Hence lies my secret weapon for
tonight.

The drinks have been flowing now and everyone's in a
good mood – Pete's wasted, Sarah's on the prowl and it
looks like someone's just about to get fired. Now's the
time. I grab Miss Kibbles from my bag and place her on
the turntable. She's so bloody good no one even notices.
So I grab the mic and shout, 'Give it up for DJ Kibbles!'
It takes a moment but everyone starts to clock on. The
place goes absolutely wild! Miss Kibbles is making 'Silent
Night' sound like flipping Massive Attack. I've got 'em in
the palm of my hands – now for the clincher. I'm digging
through the crates and there's the prime jewel itself – Ms
Dynamite 'Booo!' As I take it out the sleeve, something
drops on the floor... It's a photo of me and Rich at
Ministry...he's wearing that gold Moschino jacket...we were
just laughing about it the other day. I still remember how
he'd let me wear it on the way home. How he'd always
ask me to come to his cos he didn't want to leave Miss
Kibbles alone...but he did. He left her. He said he wouldn't,

but he did. He said everything would be alright, that he'd get better and life would be normal again. That he didn't need to speak to anyone, he just needed time. But time went on and he became so different – he was so quiet. I lost him long before I got that call when they said he was... He lied. He left that bloody cat and now I'm the one that's got to feed it. I'm the one that's stuck with all these fucking records and I don't know what else to do but play them...cos what do you do when the music stops?

Don't Say Anything

Ayesha Manazir Siddiqi

> **An Indian woman has a sexual awakening. Age stated in monologue as mid-twenties.**

LAILA, an Indian woman somewhere in Bihar, mid-twenties.

I... I can't believe we just did that. I'm serious, stop grinning. Oh god. You know, whatever you do, you can't say anything. You know that, right?

I have never done anything like this before. Shit.
Was it... OK? No, no. Don't answer that. I don't wanna know.
I've never done that before. Like, literally. I have never done this before. Did you know that?
Ten years of marriage and I've never done that before.
Not like that.
What kind of God....

I wasn't even sure anything was wrong. Can you believe that? I mean. In the beginning, when I first married him, I knew. I'm not stupid I know what's supposed to go where, you know? But after a while, I just thought, accha, chalo, this must be the way it's meant to be, for most people. The way I'd dreamed it would be was story books, fantasy. Or sometimes I felt like, if I had been different, like prettier or more hospitable or something, maybe it would have happened? And I tried so hard to be prettier, you know? Waxing, bleaching, all that chutiyapa. But, I don't know, maybe it made the problem more obvious, so the more I tried, the meaner he got. I bought this thing once, this little, you know, see-through thing, and I walked into the room with it on, and he looked at me, and burst out laughing. He did that on purpose, right? Just to... I don't know...crush me.

But you know where I always knew? In my dreams. In my dreams, he would do it right. You don't need to do it to know what it feels like to do it right. Ahh. Why am I even telling you this? You must think I'm so naïve. Vaisay, how do you know? I mean, how do you know how to do it so right? Loads of practice, right? Don't answer, it's none of my business. Better to not talk about it. It's over now.

But when did you start thinking about it? Like, when you asked to stay, did you know he would be away? No. Don't say. I don't want to know. It's just, you can't help thinking, that it's probably not that good with everyone, right? Like, it takes two? And so...if it was that good, maybe... that's some kind of sign from God, huh? I'm being silly. I don't even know what I'm saying.

It's just...do you know what it feels like, to have a longing for something, for years and years, and to think that what you long for just doesn't exist? And then, you find out. No, actually, surprise, fooled you, it does. Here's a taste. Just a small one though. Just so you know what you're missing. Is it better to know, you think, or to never have found out?

Say something.

Douglas

Mahad Ali

> **A politician defends their actions and who they are. For ages 25 and above.**

DOUGLAS does his tie up and moves to the front of the podium to address Parliament.

War! My Right Honourable Friends, we are in a state of war! War has been declared upon our nation by those that despise our way of life and our freedoms. By those who have the means and what they believe to be the justifications to hurt the British people. As Prime Minister it is my duty to protect the realm from all real and potential threats that endanger the lives of our civilians. Now I do not seek to apologise to those in the House that see war as barbaric and evil. Many wars have been fought on just grounds against evil and threats of terror, which know or understand no other response than force. This is why I took the steps to declare a state of emergency and martial law, giving citizens a curfew of ten p.m. These steps were to ensure we route out the threat and make our streets safe again.

Pause – deep breath.

Less than a month ago – I was elected on a platform of hope and change. Many invested their hopes in me... especially the young.

But when the facts change, as they did with this bombing, so must one's opinion. To do what is necessary to protect our beloved country.

My Right Honourable Friend and leader of the opposition will allude to my speeches where I speak of democracy, the rule of law, international norms and conventions. He will say that my behaviour defies such norms and that we must solve matters through diplomatic means.

He now proposes a vote of no confidence in me for doing the very things and taking the very measures he has always advocated.

I say how dare he! When he was in power for four years, he took decision after decision that put our country in this place, in the first place! Set us on a collision course with other countries and put our national security at risk. And now he sits here claiming to be the Dalai Lama.

It is no coincidence since the bombing; that insinuations have been made through our press and media that this attacker looks like me; that he originates from the same part of the world as me – that we must in some perverse universe be in some form of collusion...

To me these rumours indulged in and propagated by the opposition party speak against our values as a country and as people. Where they seek to divide us along racial, ethnic and religious lines – seeking to appeal to the worst part of men – hate!

So when you vote, know that you are voting on our values. But I do not seek nor want your vote, unless you are willing to up hold these values of tolerance and respect, not a campaign of lies built up against me. The choice is yours...

> *DOUGLAS leaves the podium and walks out of the room.*

Dream Big

Unique Spencer

> **A man at the job centre has high hopes of becoming a pilot. Age stated in monologue as 35 years old.**

DENISON, 35, sits on a chair waiting nervously. He wipes his forehead with a flannel. He has paperwork that looks very old and unorganised.

The person he's been waiting for sits down to join him.

I just wanna dream big...

So, I've filled out all the paperwork and brought all my ID and documents...oh before we get started I just wanted to let you know that I've recently found out I'm a father. Just so you know, I haven't lied on the form, I just didn't know until now. It's really important to me that I get this job. I'm not saying there's anything wrong with people flipping burgers, but I need more... I wanna be a father who provides...wow...first time I've ever said that...

> *DENISON wipes his forehead with a flannel.*

> *DENISON smiles to himself and starts to look through his paperwork.*

I have all my carpentry certificates. Most of the skills I've learnt are transferable. I know I'm gonna have to take a few more courses and stuff but flying is in my blood. When I was a kid my father brought me the uniform. I even got to fly my own plane, not a real one but I did go on one of them simulation planes at the funfair. I just remember the feeling of being free. And in the background was this beautiful smell of candy floss.

DENISON smiles to himself.

Ever since that day I've spent the last twenty-five years watching them go up and down which sort of resembles my life. Now I just wanna be levitating in the sky so high that I'm only competing with the birds.

DENISON wipes his head with his flannel.

So, erm how long until you think you could get me an interview? I'm sure there's not many people coming to the job centre asking to become a pilot.

Drive

Hassan Abdulrazzak

> **A young scientist is questioned about his latest experiment designed to change the world. Age stated in monologue as 24 years old.**

It's not my fault... Yes, technically it was my project. But you see... If you stop interrupting me. I don't care that this is a parliamentary hearing. I'm the CEO of GeneDreams. What are you? A third rate MP in a Marks & Sparks suit. No, no, no. I wouldn't say millions will die... thousands, maybe... I'm not being blasé about it... Oh come off it, you've really lost the argument when you start comparing people...start comparing *me* to Nazis.

I'm perfectly calm. Perfectly calm. Perfectly calm. It just bothers me that you don't get it. Scientists have been dreaming about this for years. To genetically engineer mosquitoes so they wouldn't carry the malaria parasite. But there wasn't a good way to do it. Say you make a mosquito that was a mutant, that didn't carry the parasite. What do you do next? If you release it into the wild, it will mate with the native population and that mutation will be lost. If you go into a village that has say 10,000 mosquitoes, you'd have to release 100,000 mutant mosquitos to make any dent into the native population. You'll end up with a lot of unhappy villagers cursing you and your ancestors to hell.
But I developed a new technology where I can make just

two mutant mosquitos and that pair has the ability to spread its genes to all the population in record time. The technology is called Gene Drive. And yes I'm one of its pioneers. GeneDreams wasn't just any start up. We shot up the FTSE 100 like a line of coke shooting up a nostril. I am twenty-four years old and I have a team under my command made up of thirty scientists. Many of them are twice or three times my age. Do you know what my motto is madam? 'I really don't think that's good enough'. That's what I tell my staff. That's what I tell my girlfriend when she screws up a new dish. That's what I told my younger brother when he only got accepted at Oxford and not Cambridge. 'I really don't think that's good enough' is the motto that got me where I am today.

So yes, we made the mutant mosquito and we released it into the wild. And by Darwin, it worked. I mean in about a month, we eradicated malaria entirely. Did you read about our success in *Time* magazine? Did you see the reports on the BBC?

Yes, there was a glitch, I admit. But it had nothing to do with me. I have tried to explain that to you now almost three times in this hearing. It's really tiresome for me to deal with people with low IQ. Yes, I am calling you stupid. The very fact you have to ask me that after I said 'low IQ' proves that you are.

I repeat. It was not me who carried out the experiment. I have a team of thirty people. Yes, I know I said that already but you are clearly not hearing me even though this is supposed to be a 'hearing'. What are their salaries? What does that have to do with anything? Sure they work eighteen, twenty hours a day but that's the norm in science at this level. We pay them enough. Well, they're not starving, let's just put it that way. One of them made an error in the way she designed the Gene Drive. So now, unexpectedly the mutation has jumped to us...you know what it means... I wouldn't be here before you if you didn't know that. You want to hear it from me? You really are very tiresome. Fine, fine, it means that many children born now will die before they reach adulthood. Yes, well like I say it wasn't my fault. I couldn't get into the nitty gritty... I'm a very busy man. Just last month I was at a conference in the Bahamas giving the keynote speech and the month before that I was at a conference in the Maldives and before that in the French Riviera. I can't be expected to know the minutiae of every project I supervise, can I? I am more of the big picture guy. You don't run a FTSE 100 company if you are not the big picture guy. It's the reason why I am wearing an Armani suit and you are in Primark.

The damage? We are working on a paper now to estimate the damage, scientifically and accurately. No, no, I will not be drawn into numbers. Look, we won't feel the loss for some years. Frankly if we think about this rationally, this could be the best thing for the planet. This could really reduce the carbon footprint. There will be more housing for everyone, less traffic... You really don't think my argument is good enough? Tough. The mosquitos are already out there. My advice to you madam, my advice to everyone in this room is: enjoy your children whilst you have them. Oh and stay away from salmon. But that's a story for another hearing perhaps.

Dwayne

NSR Khan

> **A single father learns how to make gender neutral fairy cakes with his young daughter. For ages 18 and above.**

(In a baby voice.) 'Daddy what are you doing?'

This is what I'm doing: *(Claps his hand over his mouth, for a second, then lets his hand fall naturally, so that he can carry on speaking.)*

Because if I don't do this: *(Replacing hand over mouth, and then letting it fall.)*

Then this will happen: *(DWAYNE lets out an angry roar.)*

And this: *(letting out a second roar)* is not supposed to happen. Ever. In front of my Princess Keisha. And I suppose Jermel. But is he too tiny, maybe, to care? You know what I mean?

It's not like, I don't know that, but you know some people, well mostly women actually, they do like to remind me, like a lot.

(In a baby voice.) 'Daddy this is gonna take ages!'

 Yeh. It will. It's long. It always is.

BBC Food website says that fairy cakes take less than thirty mins prep. Tops.

Keisha and me, well really, just me...we've been making

fairy cakes for, like, a month. It's a whatsit...bonding
activity? Fairy cakes for my fairy princess. You know
what I mean?

Our prep time? Sixty mins. If we're lucky.

Cos I'm imagining that the woman who wrote the
recipe...cos it must have been some woman, maybe a
career woman with a nanny.

That she wasn't, with one hand, putting Jermel in his
playpen,

changing his nappy,

checking for new domestic painting jobs on Rated
people.com.

I'm a 'rated' painter, you know?

Clearing out Keisha's book bag and...

and...preparing fairy cakes. With the other.

Today though'...our sixty mins target? Not happening.
Not even close.

Cos I'mma gonna be doing this: *(Hand on mouth, then
lets it fall.)*

So, this: *(Roars.)*

Don't happen.

You know what I mean?

But you don't, do you? Know what I mean. Cos even if I tell
you. Well you're not gonna get it. Cos I wouldn't get it.

I mean if this weren't my life, I wouldn't get, why I'mma doing this: *(Hand over mouth, then removes it to carry on speaking.)*

(In Keisha's voice.) 'Silly Daddy. Not fairy cakes. Miss said cupcakes. We've got to make cupcakes.'

That's why. Right there. Keisha said it.

I've been praying, as in please Almighty God hear my prayer and don't let Keisha take their side. Don't let her say 'cupcakes' out loud. In case this *(roars)* happens.

Please Keisha, don't Google cupcakes. She is. She really is googling.

I don't want no 'Miss said...cupcakes today'.

'Miss', Keisha's teacher, actually, she's not the worst. Of the women. The women who like to remind me of stuff.

Until today, that is.

And I get it. I do. They're all...all the women, you know social workers and that...they're trying to help.

But people like me, like us, you know? With a trade, no criminal record, never on benefits. We don't need help.

Well why would I need help, unless?

Unless,

the one woman who should be here, who should be making cupcakes instead of me...unless,

she hadn't just,

'Oh I'm going uni.'

Who does that?

What mother does that...gone uni. And never come back.

'I deserve a career, Dwayne.'

She had a career. Right here. No? Don't you t'ink?

The most important one of all. How can there be any, like, more important job than that? Bringing Keisha and Jermel up strong? But somehow even though' she did the worst t'ing.

Up and left. Them with me. Everything is down to me.

So here we are: Jermel in the playpen, Keisha and me in the kitchen, fighting over damn cupcakes. Why?

'Miss' says...

I can't even say it... I know what it means...but I, actually t'ink it's gonna hurt, if I actually even say it out loud:

'Miss' says fairy cakes are *(pause)* like, 'gender specific'.

And that we...me and Kiesha, in our bonding, we should be focusing on *(pause)* gender neutral baked goods. For Kiesha's sake.

Oh my days! Can't they see? For Keisha's sake?

For Kiesha's sake I would make any kind of cakes:

Girl cakes.

Boy cakes. Hell even transgender cakes. Any kind.

I do get it. But do they?

That like any mum, cos it turns out, I'm Keisha's mummy as well as daddy, now.

I'm gonna *(starts to roar but stops mid-roar and then out of the blue, he smiles)* well, let off some steam, sometimes.

That don't mean that I don't get it.

Course Keisha's gonna be a woman one day, too. Maybe she'll bake cakes with her babies, one day, too. Maybe she won't. Maybe a woman who goes uni, one day, too. Maybe a woman who has a career, one day, too. Maybe a fact checking kind of career, one day, too. A 'googling the hell out it', kind of career, one day, too.

Like she's doing, well...today.

Turns out, I don't know, if you know this, but Princess Keisha's research is just in.

Turns out, ooh just let me enjoy the moment: turns out fairies, turns out fairies...oh my days, I can't even say it.

Thank you, Princess Fairy Keisha for this fact: fairies have what is called a 'non-binary gender identity', you know what I mean?

Let me just pop that in the oven, right now!

Falling Off the Edge

Tuyen Do

> **A wife, long suspecting that her husband is a paedophile, turns him in to the police. Age stated in monologue as 50 years old.**

SYIA, fifty, psychologist

Family home. Talking to her husband. She's just come home from work. Still has her shoes and coat on.

Did you know, given all the information about their genetic make up, including the increased probability of cancers, diabetes and heart disease – death sentences in other words – people still don't change their behaviour. They carry on smoking and drinking and stuffing their faces like they were never given the choice to stop it. Why do you think that is? Is it because we're all optimists? Or is it because we cannot change?

I spend my days helping people find answers to their questions. The things that plague them, day and night, their demons. I search with them, through the dark, guiding them with the little light I have... And sooner or later we find a path they can tread, one step at a time. A path that stops them from falling off the edge.

I've been trying. Really trying. I've been waiting for some sort of sign, something to say to me, to say to me... you can understand...you can find a way through...

But here are things that cannot be fixed like this. Some things I can't...

Don't touch me! Don't you, you...you...

I'm not here to help you. You are not my patient. You are my...was my...oh fuck...

...I feel disgusting.

The images...they start. They start and they don't stop. Terrible...disgusting things you may or may not have done.

You have a disease Michael and it's not going away. You are sick. Very very sick.

You're a monster.

People don't change. They don't.

They hear sirens.

They have your laptop. That's where I've been. I'm sorry Michael. I'm so so sorry. Don't run. If you have any love for me, please don't run.

Fish Out of Water

Rabiah Hussain

> **A bullied school girl out on a trip decides to not return home with the rest of her class. For school ages.**

I'm trying to drown out the sound of Mrs Brendon shouting from across the beach. 'The coach is leaving! Get yourself down here, young lady! Right now!' It's easy to ignore her because my main concern isn't her. It's Tara sitting at the back of the coach, waiting for me to get on.

Pause.

I don't really know how I got here. To this spot. Facing the water, bare feet in the wet sand. I sat in a corner, on a rusty deckchair, fully clothed, watching everyone, and dreading the stones and dirt Tara kept throwing at me... she says she's going to cut my hair off on the way home.

Pause.

Tara has been in my life since I was five. Same primary school. Same secondary school. And now same college. When I was little, she used to pinch me. As I got older, the pinches turned to punches. But what scared me the most was that one day, she would feel the ridges and scales on my legs. The legs I've spent a lifetime trying to hide from everyone. The ugliness of them. The reason I can't wear a swim suit like everyone else here today.

Pause.

'I'm going to count to five!'

Even from here I can see the big vein on Mrs Brendon's forehead popping out as she stands in front of the coach, hands on hips. Through the little windows, I can see Tara waiting for me.

Pause.

'Four!'

I know what Mrs Brendon is going to say to me. That I spent the entire day moping around and *now* I want to go for a swim? When it's time to go back home.

Pause as she notices something.

Shit! Tara is stepping off the coach. She is saying something to Mrs Brendon...

'Tara's going to help you back!' Shit! Shit! Shit! If I undress right now and walk into the water, everything will come to its rightful end. That's the only way. It's not an easy choice to make. But I'll tell you what: if I see even one person notice me on this beach. Even one person then I won't do it. I will go back...

Pause.

She's coming toward me. Her fast-paced walk is turning into a jog. She's got that evil look in her eyes and she's clearly thinking about the different kinds of physical and verbal abuse she'll inflict on me as she drags me back to the coach. But if I go into the water right now, it will all be over. All the pain. The bullying. The invisibility.

Pause.

I unzip my jeans and slowly pull them down. The cold, wet air stings me. The marks look even more prominent today. I guess it's being near water. I unbutton my shirt and throw it down. All of a sudden, I'm exposed. Every person is looking at me. At my reptile like legs. The roughness hurting their eyes. I'm probably the ugliest sight they've ever seen.

I take small steps into the water, the tide sweeping across my feet. My steps get heavier as the water is climbing higher. To my ankles. Then my knees. I can feel the change already. The tide is rushing toward me and the water is now up to my hips. I have everyone's attention: they are standing still and looking at me. Including Tara. I hold my arms up and the wave takes me.

I hear gasps. I hear panics. But...this is the truest, the realest moment of my life. I feel my scars getting bigger. Joining together. My hair gets longer. It turns a rainbow colour. My feet turn to fins and my fishtail emerges. I glide through the water, more beautiful than I've ever been in my life. The world is at its knees. Because now they know.

I'm not invisible anymore.

Foam

Ross Willis

> **A bartender watches her friend being groped in the midst of a foam party at the club they work for. For ages 18 and above.**

My best mate Stacey can do smoke tricks. Ya know like rings and giant elephants? Says if you can do smoking tricks you've got less chance of catching cancer.

She might not know about how rain works but she knows about the important things in life.

Known her all my life. When I was eight, I accidently broke this bloke's window, she took the blame. When I tried to run away from home for the night, she hid me in her closet and fed me Hobnobs.

She's brave. I ain't.

(To a customer.) I don't need to see your ID mate. Everyone looks like a serial killer in their passport photo. What you having?

Serving one more underage toddler won't make any difference.

I kid you not, the other day Barney literally let in a toddler. Wasn't paying attention, toddler just toddled on in.

Poured him a pint 'cause that's what I do.

I thought to myself I did. Ain't that a toddler?

It's getting the balance right, ain't it? Between not giving a shit and letting a toddler in. But of course, if a toddler wants to come in, starts causing a fuss just let him in. Don't get involved.

Foam party tonight. Stacey is in. Going wild. Dancing on the table. I should stop her but I love the way she dances. She's free. Bet she doesn't look like a serial killer in her passport photo.

And the foam falls.
Cloud burst of snowy suds pouring from them high heavens.
Stacey's hands flapping around to catch it like it's stardust.
And the foam falls.
My friend in the foam dancing on the table.
And the foam falls –

   Beat.

This man is touching her.
And the foam –
He keeps touching her.
And the foam –
She don't wanna be touched!
The bouncers can't see. Why can't they see this?
No one can see. Ain't nobody but me can see.
Don't get involved. This ain't you. You don't do this.
Shut them eyes tight. Clenched fists. Eyes sinking in sockets.
And the foam falls. And the foam falls. And the foam falls.
My friend struggling in the foam.
My friend drowning in the foam.
My friend being touched in the foam.

ROSS WILLIS

Soggy hand wandering and wandering.
Soggy hand on her arm, her boob.
She pulls away.
Soggy hand grabs her tighter.
Crushing the air out of her lungs.
Soggy hand now travelling places it shouldn't go.
Not there! Not there!
She's looking to me.
My friend in the foam looking to me.
I see her sad eyes staring through them soapy suds.
She's begging me and I'm begging her to stop begging me.

Gotta make a choice. Gotta make a choice. Gotta save
my friend.

I'm walking over.
Leaving that bar. Leaving that overpriced vodka.
I'm walking over.

The foam burns as it touches my skin.

I'm walking over.

My friend who took the blame.
My friend who gave me Hobnobs.

My friend in the foam.

Free

Tuyen Do

> **A mother tells her son that she finally feels free after falling in love with a woman. Age stated in monologue as 32 years old.**

JEBA is a thirty-two-year-old housewife/Instagram sensation.

She is talking to her fourteen-year-old son.

Asif? Are you asleep? I'm sorry you had to find out like that. I was going to come and talk to you... Your dad...he's having a difficult time...even I don't really understand. So I don't expect him to either...

Asif? I know you're not asleep. I'm going to come in OK? You don't have to talk to me. I'll just talk to you. Or just sit with you if you like. Like when you were little?

> *She approaches carefully. Takes him in and sits. He turns further away.*

I know I haven't been the best mum. You're so capable, I forget you're only fourteen. That's no excuse I know. I haven't been there for you. I'm sorry. I'm sorry for that. I've been sick but I'm getting better now. Much, much better. This doctor I've been talking to, she's made me realise a few things. Things that I've been keeping hidden, so it was making me ill. And now I know what it is, I'm working towards becoming better. And this is going to help me OK? Me leaving means that I can get the help I need so that I can be here for you for a long long time to come. Do you understand?

Look, your mum's not great with words but I'm going to try. I'm going to try and explain this.

You know how when you were six we signed you up to football club? You went every Saturday morning for nearly two years. You went because your friends went, and your dad liked it, and then there was the money...and that's what boys do so you went. But every Saturday morning, you had trouble getting up. Your movements would become slow, you could barely get out of bed, so your dad had to hurry you up, every Saturday. But you didn't complain because I was... well... I was ill...and it made your dad happy so you went because that's the sort of boy you are. But then you discovered dance and you realised that football was making you very very unhappy, and you came to me in tears because you thought there was something wrong with you. But there wasn't. It's just that dancing made you feel free, and football made you feel...the opposite.

I don't know if this is making any sense. What I'm trying to say to you is that, is that I've discovered my version of your dancing. Sarah is my version of your dancing. I can't believe I'm saying this out loud.

The truth of it hits her...

I love you so much. My boy. My baby boy. I know this is hard for you to hear but none of this changes the way I feel about you. There are going to be a million things running though your head, and you are going to hate me, and want to hit me and call me all sorts of names and I am ready for that. But I want you to remember this conversation. Because once that's all over, and you want to find me, I will be here for you.

Do you hear me Asif? I will be here for you.

Going to Paris

Ayesha Manazir Siddiqi

> **A woman who works for an online chat room has ambitions of a new life in Paris. For ages 18 and above.**

This is it. Chez moi! That's 'my house' in French. Next summer, you know, we're going to France, us housemates. Christie's aunt has a place we can stay in. Baguettes and wine on the Eiffel Tower, baby!

The mirror's cool, isn't it? I use it to dance practice sometimes. Hmmhmmhm *(She hums as she does a little dance in front of the mirror.)* Too sexy? Shut up. You still see me as a tom boy, that's what. She is a thing of the past, that tomboy. Hmmhmmhmm *(more dancing)*. You want some wine, hun? We've got a red here somewhere...

Uh no, not bartending anymore. I...just... I kinda found another way to make money. It's like, modeling, basically. Why's that funny? I'm actually really good at it. It's only like an online kind of gig anyway. Like...chat rooms sort of. And you do a little dance or whatever, and people come and watch, and they give you tokens, and you have a menu, like. Different tokens for different things. Yep. Something like that. You sure you don't want wine?

Ugh, Cheryl, don't be such a prude, it's not 'shady'. But yes, I do take my top off if that is what you mean. It is on the menu. Cheryl, please. What do *you* do all day? Take care of Richie basically. Yeah, you do. 'How was work, baby. You want some pasta?' I've heard you. Do you get paid for that? Loads of the men on there, they just want to talk, you know. About their mums and wives and things. I just have to be like, 'oh, honey, tell me how you feel.' *And* I get paid for that! It's about time we got paid for this shit, you know? This shit that we do anyway, every single day.

What, you're just not going to say anything now?

Look, it's not like I have some kind of *Pretty Woman* fantasy. Someone's gonna see me there and be like, ahh. Let me take care of you. No way, man. Even in the films, that only happens to the white girls. Us, we end up in the trunk of the car. Dead. Naa. My screen name's Julia Roberts on there, but that's just for a laugh.

Look, it's called working the system, hun. We try to play at their games, but we forget, we've got our own games. You're sitting at home, saving for uni, buying Richie shit. That's not how it's going to happen. My housemate, Christie, she grew up riding horses. It's not just people like that who get to go to Paris, you know? You and I, we can go to Paris too.

> **Potential ending point here if time is limited. Otherwise:**

What, you're just not speaking now?

You think you're so above it all, don't you? Well, hun... I don't know how to say this but...actually, no, it's not important. OK. If you have to know, I saw him on there.

Richie. He hangs out in those chat rooms all the time, I guess. He saw me and logged off, and I didn't think he would tell you but I just thought better you hear it from me. No hun, don't ring him. Listen. I'm going to open a bottle of wine and we'll talk about this, alright?

Hold on, let me find a good one. Christie got some nice wine from Costa Rica – she went trekking there last month. You know where that is? South America. Alrite then, here you go. OK. Now. Tell me how you feel, hun.

Gold Dust

Ross Willis

An amateur boxer finds out that his coach is gay and has to decide if he will allow this to ruin their relationship. For ages 18 and above.

You literally punched his face off.
I'm tryin' to tell him he used the word incorrectly.
YOU LITERALLY PUNCHED HIS FACE OFF!
But the word literally –
Who gives a fuck! ABA National semi-finals here we
come my son!

I like it when he calls me son. I love it when he calls me son.

Coach looks like an Asian Danny DeVito. Doesn't walk. Only
ever shuffles. No one's actually seen him move his feet.
Says I got a gift. Says it's something you can't teach.
He gives me that look a proud parent gives when their
kid draws a shit picture but that parent looks at it like
it's fuckin' gold dust.

Celebration drinks. Just one pint he says. Yeah just one
pint and fifty fuckin' shots! *Waheeeeey.*

Why'd you wanna come to this bar I say.
'Cause I'm thinkin ain't this one of *them* places.
Coach never goes to bars, always planning the next
training session.
Too late he's bolted through the door. Never seen

him move so quick, he's like some cracked out kid on Christmas day.

Inside it's like they stole all the glitter in the world and placed it in this one room. Topless men dancin' in cages.
Blokes snoggin' each other.
There's this bloke dressed up as a unicorn casually grindin' on a pole.

I kid you not.
'Cause I'm thinkin'.
Maybe.
This is a gay bar?
Nah. Nah. I mean don't get me wrong. I ain't got a problem. Nah. Nah. I ain't got a problem. Nah. *(Proudly.)*
I listen to Elton John. I recycle.
Not got a problem. Nah.
But.

Cause I'm thinkin'. They're all watchin' me.
Checkin' me out ain't they?
I've only gone and lost coach and I'm feelin' like that scene in *Jaws* where that shark is lurkin' underwater about to chew that bird's leg off.

    Beat.

Until I see coach in the corner.

Kissin' this guy.
Chewin' his face off, *literally.*

His arms around him. Gigglin'. Slow dancin' under them pink neon lights. He looks happy.
Happier than I've ever seen him.

He never told me he was...

'Cause I thought we wanted to win medals but maybe you just wanted to suck dick.
And it's like the coach I knew, the coach who did all that top bants is gone and everythin' is changed.

DING.

'FOCUS!'
ABA National Semi-Finals. This is it. Everythin' I wanted.
'FOCUS!'
Blood drippin' from my face. Puffy eyes. Sweat pourin' like a power shower.
'FOCUS!'
He keeps lookin' at me. Stop lookin' at me!
'FOCUS!'
Brain and fist ain't connectin'.
'FOCUS!'
You're not gold dust.
'FOCUS!'
You were never gold dust.
'FOCUS!'
You're just a shit picture.

Minute break. I'm slumped in the corner like some washed up whale on a beach.

He says you ain't gotta look me in the eyes but you gotta listen. You can give up on me, but I won't let you give up on yourself. Says you've got a gift my son and it's a crime if you don't use it.

I might be some limped wrist faggot but I'm capable of throwin' a punch, what about you? You're *literally* gay

119

then I ask? He nods.
He's holdin' out his hand for me to shake it and he's
lookin' at me like I'm gold dust.

A man is holdin' out his hand who kisses men and sucks
dick.
A man is holdin' out his hand who's never treated me
differently if I win or lose.
A man is holdin' out his hand who's given his entire life
to get me to this moment.

Stop literally diggin' your own grave and go out there
and win this my son, he says.

My son.

I Dream Of Drake

Tara Alexis

> **After a one night stand, a woman watches her date sleep and fantasies about a life they could have together. Age stated in monologue as around 25 years old.**

CHARLENE BLACKWELL, around 25 years old.

CHARLENE is staring intently at a guy she pulled last night. It's the morning after, or rather the afternoon after; her mystery man has been asleep for a long time. CHARLENE has showered, made brunch, prepared Monday's lesson plan for her class of nursery school children and is now lying down on the bed next to the mystery man. He wakes up.

Hi. Now that you're awake, can I ask you something? Are you a dream? Actually, wait, that's stupid; you can't be a dream, because I only dream of Drake, and you're not him. You are nice though. Still tired? You just did three big blinks but you can't to go back to sleep now – pillow talk! Do you pluck your eyebrows? Sorry, sorry, it's just that they're so perfect. Like two freshly cut gardens, or one long garden path. They make me want to *(CHARLENE takes her middle and index fingers and moves them across his face as if they were a pair of legs walking)* take a walk somewhere. I go for walks all the time with the kids. I say walks – well, I walk and push, they just sit there in their buggies and pick their noses. I do love them though, and I love my job. What do you do for a living? You look like a corporate kind of guy. Well, you did last night in your shirt and trousers, but now that you're naked you kind of look like a bartender.

Last night was really amazing, like, all of it. I don't usually throw up after sex – that was because of the tequila. Didn't put you off though, did it babe? Yuck, I hate the word babe. Don't you think it makes me sound like one the characters from *Eastenders*? 'Come here babe, I live on Albert Square babe.' Where do you live? I live...oh. Well, you know where I live! Living here's great you know.

If you ever wanted to try it, I wouldn't say no. I was joking...was I? Well yeah, both times *(CHARLENE shakes her head to suggest no she wasn't joking)*. I've always lived North. The Durojaiye's, that's my family, when they first came over to London they all settled in Peckham, except for my mum and dad. They preferred North, but one day I want to move to the country. Like, the real countryside, not Epping, and live in a village. I also dream about having my own nursery one day. So, where do you see yourself in five years' time? And do you have any hereditary diseases that would play a major factor in family planning? Sorry, sorry, it's just that last night was the best night of my life, like, so far. It was like the closest thing I've ever felt to being in love, having someone love me. I couldn't believe it when I woke up and you were still here. You even held my hand in your sleep. Do you remember? You like, turned your back on me and I thought, OK, and then you reached out for my hand and slowly moved it across your body and I thought, not another hand job bruv, it's gonna drop off! It's four o' clock in the morning, let me sleep, and then you linked your fingers with mine and I thought, this must be what husbands and wives feel like. What boyfriends and girlfriends who finish each other's sentences do. I swear I could have cried. I'm not a psycho or anything, but my heart was so full and it was real, it was actually happening, I wasn't dreaming. Drake can do one because I've got you and so I don't want you to leave, or at least if you do, you have to come back – please? So will you? Hello? *(Mystery man wakes up for the second time.)* Hi. I was just asking if you *(He begins to get dressed.)* I was just asking you...if you want to come – coffee. If you want a coffee before you leave?

In My Life

Rachel Coombe

After an inebriated out-of-body experience, a music-loving sanitation worker decides to pursue their dream of being a rock star. For ages 18 and above.

The first time it happened, I was working in sanitation, living in a studio flat with surrealist art and band posters covering every inch of the diabolical wallpaper. I didn't bother with a bed because there was no room. I slept on a futon I liberated from my mum's house.

I would wake up every morning at the crack of dawn to lug heavy bins full of other peoples' rubbish around all day. My hip flask was in my shirt pocket, filled at the beginning of the day, and all gone by lunchtime. I would sing The Beatles loudly as I stumbled around, dropping bins and spilling crap everywhere. My co-workers avoided me as much as possible. But the daily grind of being in a job that sucked my soul out of my body became too much. Fuelled with vodka, I decided to lie down for a bit. No one noticed I had gone; they were all too busy being good worker bees.

I found a gate at the side of someone's house that had been left open, and wandered into their garden, Oasis playing loudly in my headphones.

The chorus of 'Rock 'n' Roll Star' by Oasis is sung.

I was on the verge of a deep doze, when I felt the ground beneath me start to shake. Gently at first, then hard enough to make me feel seasick. I curled into the fetal position and tried not to throw up. Underneath me, the ground was burning hot. Then the sound of waves, then the warm breeze on my skin. I was on a beach, not in a scruffy garden in East London anymore and I was a slightly drunk Dorothy. I lay back on the sand, and closed my eyes, listening to the waves.

I opened my eyes and I was back in the garden, and a tall extremely sunburnt and irate woman was swearing at me in Polish. I scrambled to my feet, and made my way home in a daze.

I simply stopped showing up for work, feigning sickness at first and then not bothering to call in at all. I turned my phone off and spent my days watching Beatles documentaries and guitar tutorials on YouTube.

All I wanted was a chance at life. My mum was a painter and a musician and when I was a kid she would tell me that music was the universal language. When I suggested that the universal language was in fact mathematics, she laughed and asked me, 'Does mathematics make you feel like a rock star?'

I started seeing a counsellor and going to music therapy classes, and singing at open mic nights, where I've made some amazing friends who love to hang out and play music 'til the early hours of the morning. I've come very close to sharing my secret once or twice. Once with my counsellor and just last week, with a very handsome teacher I met at a musicians jam. Of course we spent most of the night arguing about mathematics being the universal language.

I asked him if teaching maths made him feel like a rock star. He admitted that, no, music does. So we played our guitars and we sang in harmony.

The first verse of 'In My Life' by The Beatles is sung.

Ishmael
Iman Qureshi

> **A young man thinks love is like maths and calculates that marrying a girl from Russia is his best chance of finding love. Age stated in monologue as 19 years old.**

'You WHAT?'

That's my mum talking.

I said, I'd like to invite you to my wedding.

'To who? What nonsense. How?!'

What do you mean how? I just rang up the council and they sorted it.

'No, fool. I mean – who are you marrying? Or more importantly, who is marrying YOU?!' That's my mum for you. Harsh.

'Russian girl' I say.

'Eh?!'

She's getting stressed now. From Krasnodar, I say.

'Where now?!'

She needs a visa, I need a wife. Deal done.

'What nonsense? Who says you need a wife? You're nineteen. Go sleep around a bit like a real man.' This shit again.

'Ishmael', she keeps on. 'Look at me.'

I look at her. She's got serious mum face on. The one where she wants me to share and talk about my feelings and sex life and stuff.

'What's this about?'

Look, I say. I did the calculations. So the population of Britain is 66 million. Of that 51% are women. So that's like 34 million women. And only like 13% of them live in London, so are realistic prospects for me, right? So that makes – 4.5 million women roughly right? Who are potentials.

'Okayyyyy', she says. I carry on. Of them, maybe only 10% are of an age that's appropriate to marry me right? So down to 450,000 women. She looks at me like I'm mental. I'm not mental though, so I keep going. Of those 450,000 I'm only going to be physically attracted to like what, maybe 50%? And intellectually only about 1% are probably smart enough so they don't bore me to death so that cuts it right down to 2,250. 2,250 women, that's all! And of those 2,250, who will actually be attracted to me, mum? Like seriously who?

'Ishy don't say that, you're my little prince.'

We're talking seriously buff girls. I mean, we're basically at the Rachel Riley's of this world, you know, that show you watch? Countdown? The blonde one who does the numbers?

'Oh yeah she way out of your league boy. You get those big thoughts out of your head.'

Exactly. I can see I'm getting somewhere with her now. She *is* out of my league. So say of them 2,250 Rachel Riley type girls, maybe only 0.5% find me attractive – that's eleven girls. ELEVEN! Eleven girls in the whole of the UK that I could feasibly be in a relationship with. And then there are other variables. Say half of them vote Tory – Boom, down to 5.5. And say 30% of them are just pure racist so wouldn't date a black man, boom, down to 4......

'Hold on –' Mum interrupts my flow. 'These racists. I think you will have already eliminated them when you eliminated the Tories.' Shit. She's right.

'Ah? See? Don't think your mother doesn't know nothing.' Fine. But still, I say. Five women. How am I meant to find one of these five women?!

'What about – Tinder? Everyone's doing it these days. Even me. See? But too many dick pics hah.' Information I did not need to know. Anyway listen, I say. I've got another calculation for Tinder...

'No no, please. Lord spare us all.' Mum says. 'Anyway, how do you know this girl from Krasno...'

Her name is Galina...

'Galina...how do you know she didn't vote Tory?'

They don't have Tories in Russia mum. So will you come? To my wedding?

'Ishy. What's wrong with you darling?'

Nothing. Nothing is wrong with me.

'You are a very smart boy. Too smart for me sometimes, but you can't do mathematics equations for love.'

You're wrong, I say.

'Hah. Watch your mouth. You may be a smart boy, but I am still that smart boy's mother.'

Sorry, I mumble.

'Is there an equation for how much I love you? Can you do maths on that?'

I think. So if you took all the biological parents in the world, excluded all the dads – just the mums, again 51%, then the percentage of them who'd say, aborted? Or abandoned? Or – wait, do those things cancel out love?

'Hey! Are you listening to me?' She interrupts my thoughts again. 'Look. Sometimes, I come to kiss you goodnight and your pillow – it's all wet, so I think if he was tough, he won't be sad. So I'm hard on you, I say things to make you tough. Maybe the wrong things.'

My ears are burning. I can't believe what she's saying. Admitting she's in the wrong, I mean that's like a 1% probability.

'Maybe I make you feel stupid, because I don't know how to be a good mother to you. But I do know that you, my son, are perfect. And someone will love you.'

And she hugs me. She hugs me so hard like she wants to squeeze me in half. It hurts actually. Physically hurts. I think she might actually squeeze me in half. And her shoulder is getting wet, wet from my tears, like my pillow.

And then she pushes me away – holds me at arms length. And I hope the blush hasn't come through the black of my skin...

WHACK! She smacks me over the head.

'Now cancel your wedding idiot. And don't let me hear you speak of this nonsense again.' And she marches off. Stomp stomp. Saying 'Wedding HAHHH. My son, the joker.'

My main problem now though is, what will I say to Galina?

James

Mediah Ahmed

> **A young boy wants to tell his Nigerian father that he wants to be a ballet dancer. Age stated in monologue as 17 years old.**

JAMES, 17, ballet dancer.

JAMES is in his room. His father has just arrived from Nigeria, who is downstairs.

JAMES gets a pillow and screams into it. He stops. Heavy breathing.

He goes to the mirror and takes off his top and light pink jeans to reveal a leotard. He starts doing a boxing warm up – punching into the air – one, two, three and block.

I was just fine. Everything was just fine when Mamma told me that I need to...

Because HE is here now. Why does that change anything anyway? He doesn't know who I am, and how, when he was sitting all the way in Nigeria? But he is my father and he should accept me and love me unconditionally. That's what the church teaches you, right? God, if you are listening, you know that what I am doing is right. Right?

I mean, I remember stories of how my dad would help the young and destitute, helping young boys back in Nigeria, boys who had been disowned by their families for being gay. He helped them by giving them money from the difficulty fund and giving them a roof over their heads. I was so proud of him. That's my dad. The way my mamma was going on was that if I don't stop, it could destroy this family.

No! My father wouldn't disown me over dancing, would he?

'Dance is the work of the devil.'

Dance. Devil. Am I the devil? How can something that makes me feel so good be so bad?

Er, then again he would be a hypocrite. After a little blood of Christ I've seen him do a couple of moves with Mamma.

Arghhhhhh how can Mamma do this to me?

What's the worse thing that can happen? He'll disown me. Me giving up the dance is NOT an option. He needs to know the truth. And what better time to do it than right now.

JAMES has a pretend conversation with himself.

Dad
Yes son,
I have something I need to tell you?
What son?
I love...!
Men

Arghhhhhhhhhhhh it would just be easier to come out than reveal that I love dance. Just replace men with dance. It's not that hard.

Dad. *(Pause.)* I. *(Pause.)* Love. *(Pause.)* Dance.

For real now, just bite the bullet and just come out with it.

Dad...

Jasvinder

Sumerah Srivastav

> **Jas, after realising their Umma (grandmother) is dead, confesses to her that their life they have been living has been a lie. Age stated in monologue as 20 years old.**

Present day. JAS (20) recently arrived home to their flat they share with their grandmother. JAS is a transvestite. They change out of a mini skirt and into some trousers and uses wet wipes to remove their makeup, checking their appearance in the mirror as they go.

It's me, I'm home! Guess what? We did it Umma! A hundred thousand in two weeks. Crazy henna? Even with all the bad news in the world it turns out people still do care. I never thought we would do it...but you were right, and I was wrong, there I've said it. I'm bringing you up some tea, we're going to celebrate, and you are going to love what I've got you.

You know they rang a bell in the office when we got the final donation. Like one of those school bells that you used to have, to bring in all the kids from the fields? Well now we can bring in all those women out from danger. Let them deliver their babies safely, underground.

(To themselves.) Its funny how people must hide themselves, just so they can live.

JAS takes the tea in to their Umma.

Anyway, they let us go early to celebrate so I came straight home just to come tell you...well, I had a glass of bubbly first you know, if it's going free it'd be rude not to...

JAS is greeted by the sight of their grandmother sitting still in her chair – too still.

Umma? Umma? No, please... Oh Umma...

JAS holds their grandmother's limp hand for a while then sits back.

You always knew, didn't you? You believed in the good of people, you believed in me. Always have. Couldn't you have hung on just a little longer? *(Beat.)* I'm sorry, sorry I'm being selfish. I should call Dr Aarons shouldn't I? He'll want to see you. I will, I promise. I just...one sec...

They rummage in her bag and pulls out a jewellery box.

It's a bracelet, the one with the little charms that you wanted, see? It's got a tree on it.

I got it for you. I know you like to sit here looking out the window watching the leaves be lifted by the wind. 'We're all connected into one big root'...you were my root Umma.

You sitting here and me in there trying to follow your recipes. Why didn't I write them down? You always said I should think ahead. But who wants to think ahead to...

The truth is Umma... I didn't buy the bracelet. Someone gave it to me. No, not someone...a man. A man gave me

a bracelet. Do you understand? A man I hardly know.
Do you see what I'm trying to tell you? I don't work
for The Syria Campaign Umma. I just heard about it.
I donated but... The bell was a lie, everything about me
is a lie. I wasn't there this morning and I wasn't here
either. I was with a man...being a <u>woman</u>. Dressed as one
anyway. You see I'm not who you thought I was... I'm
different. Please Umma, give me your blessing? You're
the voice inside my head. Tell me it's OK?

    Long beat.

You're right. What I am is wrong. I'm weak, <u>she</u> is weak.
I won't be weak anymore. I promise.

    Then JAS sighs, takes their mobile out and calls the
    doctor's surgery.

Hello? I'd like to report a death.

Just One More Time

Guleraana Mir

> **A blind performer pushes her dance partner to be the best. For ages 18 and above.**

SURI is sitting in a chair. She's comfortable and confident talking to someone offstage.

You should know the routine by now. You should. We've gone over it fifty-five times this week alone. Yes I've been counting, I count every step, every half step, every breath. It's how I got to where I am and I expect you to do the same. The key to delivering your best performance is to practice. I can tell you haven't been practising, your body is stiff, unsure. Your footwork clumsy and uninspired. Do it again, alone. *(Pause.).* Did I hurt your feelings? I didn't mean to. It's just – Ok, I did. I thought pushing your buttons might make you dance better. Oh come on, don't cry. You are!

I can hear it in your voice. I wasn't that mean.

Your predecessor and I, we, we had time to grow into one another. After a while nothing was difficult anymore, he simply understood.

But you and I don't have that luxury. We are five days away from the competition and I expect more. I want more. Look, I appreciate I'm not easy to work with, but you can do this. The first time we danced, I knew you'd make me look good. Without even knowing what that means, to look good. You're intuitive, graceful and we fit together. Our bodies feel right, harmonious and that's the way it should be. That's why I'm frustrated. You frustrate me – My blindness means that I see things differently, not that I can't see at all, so I have to adapt. My eyes see through a pin hole, the rest of me sees through my hands, my skin, through my feet. And when I dance, you guide me, I see through you. Close your eyes, listen. Listen to the sound your feet make as they move, listen to how your breath speeds up as you jump and becomes more shallow as we rest. I learnt by feeling each position in my limbs. My teacher moved me from a plie into third position, pushed me, stretched me and through her guidance I learnt to trust my own body. Now I put that trust in you – the circular nature of relationships.

Do you know you have a smell? Everyone has one – don't worry, it's a nice smell. It took me a while to adjust but I've become accustomed to it. It lingers, and often I smell it last thing at night. I find it comforting. Sometimes, once you've gone I find myself searching for traces of it in this room. I know I was harsh before, I was trying to say you can do this. Yes you can. It's more than that. I. I'm trying to say – Do you trust me?

Let's go again. Just one more time.

Kick Off/Bake Off

Titilola Dawudu

> **A boy is torn between his love of football and his love of baking. For school ages.**

A football is somewhat away.

I flip it so it lands nicely. This one's gonna be good. I've got people who love what I do. They want more. I take my time. I have a certain finesse. A certain style. One day you'll see me on TV, cheering me on. Wanting me to do well. I'll be everywhere, doing what I do best. But what is that though? You see, I want both: I want to be a football player. And I also want to be a baker.

> *Gets football and kicks football gently between his feet.*

Listen, listen – don't look at me up and down like that with all your judge-y expressions on your faces. I know it's not what you'd expect me to say. I've always been pushed into doing sports, all us black boys were, and as soon as a ball touched my feet – that was it: I was there. I was there every day playing football. I joined every team I could. I practiced – in the rain, when it was boiling hot – it didn't matter.

Then one day, my mum says that I have to come with her to work. She was doing this 'bringing young people to learn a skill from an old person' thing.

Does some kick-ups.

I was paired with Doreen. I didn't mind really. She seemed nice and she didn't smell bad and she still had all her teeth. I think. I actually don't know, but they didn't fall out once, so I think they were hers. She – like you – gave me one look and I know what she was thinking. So I did what my mum told me to do; I smiled at her. Course she warmed up to me. She showed me how to make lots of things, breads, cakes, how to know when to open the oven – too soon and something wouldn't rise properly, or wouldn't cook evenly. Too late and, well – it would just burn, wouldn't it? Me and Doreen got along.

Stops the kick-ups and lets ball roll away.

She told me I had 'the knuckles to knead'. We'd be side by side. Me here. Ol' Doreen there. She'd let me make mistakes, she'd say, 'come on, show 'em to me.' And I'd hold up my hands, blow on my magic knuckles and get back to it.

I work hard, I wanted to impress her. She told me I could be on TV. She said I was better than the one with the lisp or the one that swears a lot. We'd sit and eat what we made, but I'd always bring some home for my mum. Mum liked that I was not just all about football. She liked that I liked something else. But I didn't just like it – I loved it.

Gets football and holds it in his hands.

So that brings me back to my problem. I'm good at football. My coach thinks I can get scouted next week

141

when Fulham comes to see our match. And I really want to play for a team like Fulham. I really do. But I know that won't leave time to bake.

And play football. And bake. My hands or my feet? I can make a soufflé rise as well as I can make a ball fly in the goal.

> *Starts kicking a ball around as though someone is trying to tackle him.*

Come on then, come to me, tackle. You can't can you? 'Cause I'm the best. Better than Henri. Better than Messi.

> *He stops with the ball and takes a timer out of his pocket (or phone/watch alarm beeps).*

My Viennese Whirls are done.

Laddie
Sumerah Srivastav

> **An Indian soldier, long dead, recounts his time in the First World War. Age stated in monologue as 19 years old.**

23 July 1918. Royal Flying Corps pilot Laddie (19) at his barracks for 40 Squadron in France.

It's like a ghost town in here...where is everyone? Have they given up and thrown in the proverbial towel? Ha! Unlikely. McElroy would never allow it. 'Fight to the death', that's what he would say. *(Beat.)* Well, mission accomplished Sir.

They must be out on a run. Tell the truth if I were alive I'd be back out there with them like a shot.

Ah! There he is, and not too happy by the looks of it. Don't worry Captain I'm not soft enough to mistake it for grief on my account. I know that look, you're angry. Probably some new recruit not listening, talking back. That was me a month ago. Has it really been just a month? I walked in here thinking I was the saviour of the Flying Corps. 'Gutsy as a gamecock' isn't that what you said? Quickly found me out though didn't you Sir. Nervous, awkward and scared was your summation. No one really saw me as a fighter pilot except you. I owe you Captain, I wouldn't have even lasted the month I did if it weren't for you. Although you probably haven't

given me a second thought since I was shot down. Out
with the old, in with the new. On to the next green pilot
to turn into a man. I remember you used to say, 'The
controls of an aircraft are like a woman. Be gentle in
their handling.' Women? Who had the time? I set out
to kill Huns and that I did. Ten kills in thirteen days.
Not bad. With so much death there is little room for
anything else, until of course, you are greeted by your
own death...

So here I am. Back again. I know full well that if you
could see me now you would say 'Get over it and get
on with it' and I would Captain I would. Except there's
one woman I made a promise to, an honest one, to my
sister Leila. You see when I first started at 56 Squadron
I promised I would send her an RFC broach. Silly really
but there it is. Thing is I forgot as brothers do and she
was not pleased as sisters so often are. Then when I
joined the 40th and well we got busy didn't we? But
now I need your help to do one last thing. Find her letter
Captain. Send her the broach that I promised. Please?

   LADDIE sighs in futility.

What are you writing anyway? More flight plans? You
know in the end when we're out there we're all fighting
blind anyway. Killing on instinct like you taught me.
Does that make me a good pilot or a good murderer?
I'm not sure which I am or if it was worth it but I am
certain I'm still a son and a brother.

Come on George, we were friends I thought. 'Foreigners
together' remember? An Irishman and an Indian fighting
for the English. At least go through my things. I would

do the same for you if the tables of fate were turned. Oh really George you are a bore, let some other hack do the paperwork.

LADDIE looks over George's shoulder and reads what he writes.

'The Air Ministry'? You despise those paper pushers, what business do you have with them? 'The Distinguished Flying Cross...' Good Lord. You mean to make me an Ace? I joked about being the Indian Albert Ball but surely that's not possible...

(Reading.) 'Bold, gallant and brave son and brother... I'm sorry for your loss.'

I'm sorry too. Thank you, George. The Flying Cross beats a broach any day of the week. With that, I'll be remembered, won't I?

Notes

This monologue is based on a real historical figure named Lieutenant Indra Lal Roy, also known as 'Laddie'. He was born in Calcutta, India on 2nd December 1898 and was educated in England at St Paul's School when war broke out in August 1914. Roy was one of the first Asian officers to be accepted by the Royal Flying Corps in 1917.

He was killed when his S.E5a was shot down by Fokker D VIIs of Jasta 29. He was nineteen years old. On 21 September 1918, Laddie was declared India's first flying 'ace' and posthumously awarded the Distinguished Flying Cross.

Lights Out

Tara Alexis

> **A woman training to be an infantry soldier admits to the assessor that she is afraid of the dark. Age stated in monologue as 23 years old.**

SHEL, 23 years old.

SHEL's second day at the British Army Assessment Centre; she is sat at a desk opposite Mr Phillips, her assessor. Having completed the physical and mental aspects of the assessment, she is now having her face-to-face interview.

I performed fourteen heaves. Did they tell you that? Did the PTI overseeing the fitness test tell you that? *(Pause.)* I see myself in a close combat role, within the infantry. I'm physically able. *(Pause.)* What motivates me on a daily basis is... I think the responsibilities of an infantry solider are... I just, I just need...a drink. *(SHEL pours herself a glass of water.)* I am prepared; please don't mistake my nerves for lack of preparation. I want this and I am happy to talk about myself and my family and my career aspirations. I knew that would be a part of the face-to-face interview. *(Pause.)*

And then there's this silence. And he wants me to fill it and I want to fill it, only I didn't want to talk about last night, but I knew I had to – It's happened before. Once or twice. It's not great, but I manage. Like someone with an unusual allergy, or a phobia of spiders you just avoid spiders. It's nothing.

I'm confident –
I was cleared in my medical. I am physically able.
He stares at me. I wasn't sure what he wanted me to say. An explanation, an apology?
Either one is an admission of failure and I can't fail,
I have to pass. We sat there in silence some more, then I surrendered –
I can explain, Sir...
My mind becomes a blizzard of excuses, of reasoning both rational, and irrational. I wish to God I could blame last night on some trauma or medical condition or one off panic attack, but I know deep down that this thing I'm dealing with lurks in the shadows of my day to day and has done since I was a little girl. Most grow out of it, but I grow with it– this fear I can't seem to shake. I'm twenty-three years old, other girls my age have a boyfriend and maybe a kid, or they've travelled, breathed the air of a county different to the one they were born in – I'm afraid of the dark–
I can explain, Sir... I will explain but please, please just give me a chance to show you that I can do this. I'm smart, I have a clean record and I'm passionate about serving my country. That has got to mean more than some little episode in the dorms last night when the lights went out. I will serve with strength and integrity. To me Sir, the army means growth and adventure and finding my place in the world. Like, this morning, in the Jerry Can test, I was told that my grip strength ranks amongst the highest recorded at this test centre ever.

TARA ALEXIS

I was made for this; I fit this life. With your instruction
and the guidance of the officers I can continue to
improve on my strengths, work on my weaknesses and
overcome my fears, my fear, of the dark.

Looking to the Future

Stefanie Reynolds

> **A beautician is watching a news report and gets distracted whilst waxing a client. For ages 18 and above.**

Beauty salon. Fumni, a bubbly beautician, is waxing a client. News report on in the background. First person to die from a virus originated from a duck.

And if you could start on your stomach please. Thank you. And then place your hands here. On the bum cheeks, exactly. Please, don't look so nervous. The bum is the least painful part. Two years I've been at this salon and another year at a different salon. I've seen it all. Nothing fazes me any more.

Sorry is that distracting you? I can turn the channel over if you like? It's terrible isn't it? Apparently this is the first virus that is untreatable. Imagine that?

You can turn on your back now. Brilliant. Feet together. Exactly, spread yourself girl. *(Laughs. The client doesn't.)* Sorry.

Apparently they are trying to kill as many of the ducks as possible, to stop the disease from spreading. But they won't be able to reach every duck, surely? Some say it's already too late, what with that man being the first to die from it. I guess we know now never to feed ducks!

She giggles.

That poor man. It's like something out of a film, isn't it? You have to admit, it is quite exciting. Not his death, obviously. That's tragic. But the idea of these diseased, disfigured ducks wiping out human existence is *bonkers*.

Place your hand here, brilliant.

Sometimes I feel sick. And my nails grow too long. And I develop a rash on my left thigh. And that's when I know. That is when I suspect, can feel something. Something huge. Happening all around us. It sounds mad that doesn't it? But I get those – symptoms – and then some sort of event happens.

Try not to wriggle.

Last time it was the earthquake in Argentina and before that the Tsunami in Chile. My symptoms arrived and so did the tragedies! I don't know why it always has to be something bleak, but it just happens that way. Everyone would think I was mad, obviously, if I told anyone, but it's a feeling, you know? But that's the problem. The "feelings" are never specific. It's just a feeling that something bad is going to happen. Previously natural disasters, but clearly nothing is safe.

Pause.

Or maybe something bad is destined to happen everyday? And I should just get this rash checked out and my nails cut. Maybe we're all mad and it's not just me. Maybe I watch too many Stanley Kubrick films. Maybe the world is bad and scary and I'm just a beautician trying my best to make a difference, and feel important by giving myself this – these 'feelings.'

I'm sorry. This isn't what you asked for is it? *(Laughs. Looks at customer's waxed area.)* Oh shit. This isn't what you asked for. I'm so sorry. I've given you a Hollywood instead of a Brazilian. I'm so sorry. I got distracted and then – it's OK. You don't have to pay! Or, wait, no, I'll give you discount – well I mean, I'm not really allowed to give a discount, it has to be authorised by my manager and this is the third time I've done this so she might fire me so actually would you mind just not saying anything and paying full price? It'll grow back. And a Hollywood is very on-trend at the moment... I can feel it! Ha.

Maya
Paula David

> **A mother records a message on her phone to her son she gave up. For ages 35 and above.**

MAYA is walking. She has been walking for miles. She walks the length of the stage goes off and comes back repeatedly. The third time she is exhausted, but she doesn't want to sit down. She pulls her phone from her bag and begins to scroll through numbers. She contemplates dialling several. Eventually she stuffs the phone back in her bag in frustration. She puts the bag on her shoulder and starts walking again, finally coming to a stop with her phone in her hand.

It's Feb 20th, two a.m. and I've been eighteen months, three weeks, three days and twelve hours without you Kashvi.

I remember whispering your name the first night we spent together. I watched you sleep and whispered Kashvi, Kashvi. I was waiting for your eyes to open and for you to instantly know who I was. In that moment I would be overwhelmed with love for you and you would know I was your mother.

The moment never came. I wasn't overwhelmed with love and you don't know your mother.

Something I'm supposed to have in me isn't there. Our

first months were spent with me desperately trying to find, to feel, to know this invisible love.

I could only feel the weight of your need, the force of your call, piercing every moment.

If you are listening to this it probably means I gave up looking. I never found the moment, you didn't become my reason for being. You should feel lucky, that I didn't continue, we would both be broken. You will have had my mother and your father for the past eighteen years without the pain of daily rejection from me. I guess that is my gift to you. My absence has given you the love you deserve. I hope that your grandmother has seen fit to give you this message so that it is the first thing you hear on the morning of your eighteenth birthday.

Mia

Paula David

A young girl tells a police officer in detail how she stabbed her teacher. For school ages.

MIA is wearing her school uniform. And is sitting on a chair, at an interview table, in a police station, facing the audience.

...can't believe how easy it was. I'm not bragging, it's just...you know you think it will be hard, you work yourself up for it and then...

MIA examines her clothes and hands carefully.

Not a fucking mark on me. Look at my nails, got 'em done this morning, not a scratch.

...sorry officer that sounds bad, it's just that I did my homework you know, thought about all the angles, it's all about seeing the detail, building a picture. The right picture for Mr Davis and knowing when to execute the final stroke, if you need to. To be honest I didn't think I'd need that final stroke, with all the prep work in class, he's been my science teacher since september, my girls helped me, it seemed like it was in the bag, you know. The picture was crystal. Don't mess with Mia!

The policeman speaks.

He was pushing me, thought he could push me, well now he knows.

The policeman speaks.

I didn't have to give myself up you know officer. I could 'ave just walked away and no one would know it was me.

The policeman speaks.

Well, 'cause I kinda wanted everyone to realise my skill.

MIA pulls out an imaginary bloodied knife to demonstrate.

You see, you go in under the ribs and hook downwards.

MIA demonstrates and looks back towards the door she came through.

Thought I wouldn't be strong enough to get it in there, didn't you Mr Davis? Anger gives you strength you know. You should have seen how wide his eyes were when I twisted the knife. If you've got it in the right place you'll be able to twist it. It was the pulling out that was difficult. I had to stand on his chest and use both hands. Thats how things got a bit messy.

As MIA looks down to demonstrate she sees two specks of blood on her shoes. She becomes instantly hysterical.

I'm sorry, I made a mess, there's blood on me, just like there was blood on his hands.

I don't know how it happened. I was just talking to him and I just stabbed him.

The policeman speaks.

No doctors I'm not gonna let them pump me full of shit again.

I was just talking to him, and I just stabbed him.

Get my Nan, she'll tell you I'm not crazy! Please officer.

The policeman speaks.

He can't be, I'm telling you, there's blood, look at the blood.

The policeman speaks.

MIA stands up.

Ok I'll show you, I'll take you there.

The policeman speaks.

I'm telling you the truth.

The policeman speaks.

He can't be you're lying.

MIA looks towards the door in shock.

Mr Davis?

My Father's Son

Femi Keeling

> **A bitter and resentful man stands over the body of his dead father. For ages 18 and above.**

FERGUS is in his father's flat, standing over his father's body, which is still warm.

This is my second time watching someone die. Second time I've seen the colour slowly leave someone's face and the life behind their eyes go with it. I've got his eyes, Mum always said. I forgot to check.

I know I've got his hands. When he held them up, pleading, I noticed that the tips of my little fingers bend inwards in exactly the same way. Before today I could only remember what his hands looked like in a fist. Like the fourth time I saw him beat her; when he left her lips so swollen she couldn't talk. She never listened, he said. So he made it so she'd have to.

He looks like he's sleeping. If you didn't know him you'd think he might be sleeping but I remember that he snores. I remember when Mum woke me up in the middle of the night, her index finger pressed against her purple lips so I didn't make a sound, we used his snoring for cover. Walked when he breathed in, froze when he breathed out, emptied the money box when he breathed in, froze when he breathed out, closed the front door behind us when he breathed in, ran like hell when he breathed out.

Mum once said I'd be the death of her. Said looking after me was like trying to put a bang back in a firework. She said I'd let her down – that I'd promised her the last time they had to call her at work and tell her to come and get me that I'd stop fighting. I didn't mean to break the promise, it wasn't up to me; being the new boy in a new school in a new town meant I had to defend myself. I tried to tell her but she was too angry to listen. That's when she told me I was my father's son. But I wasn't. I'm not. Cos I never hit the girls at school that gave me trouble, and I never hit her.

He heard through a friend that Mum had died and he wanted to see me. That's what his Facebook message said. I wanted to see if I could see me in him. He said he was sure us being together again is what Mum would've wanted. I know what she wanted. She wanted to be hit by a bus. Something quick and merciful. Not something like breast cancer, no she'd suffered enough. I heard her praying to God in the hospice, asking him to spare her the pain and end her life but – well there's no God is there? No one was listening.

When he opened his front door he opened everything up. Same flat. Same table I used to hide under. Same corners I tried to disappear into. He started off saying he was sorry but before long he was saying that thing again, that thing about her not listening, that she was really to blame, that it wasn't up to him. Well it wasn't up to me: it's these hands, these hands that ball up into fists that look just like his. When he was begging me to stop hitting him he sounded just like me. Or is it when I used to beg him to stop hitting her I sounded just like him? Well, we sound like each other, when we're begging. And just like him, I didn't stop. I blacked his eyes like when he hit her the first time, I kicked him while he was down like the second time, I stamped on him like the third time, and punched him until his lips split open like the fourth time. And I kept punching, I kept punching until he was unconscious, I kept punching until I wasn't like him, I kept punching until I became my own man. Cos he's never killed someone.

My Mate Bean

Ross Willis

> A schoolboy is peer-pressured into mis-
> treating a homeless man he calls his friend.
> For school ages.

He sits there outside Tescos in thirty degrees wearing his fancy veterans coat and beanie. He always wears it! Mental!

Bushy grey beard... Medals shinin' in the sun. And dressed for winter in the summer. That is my mate Bean for you.

'The Queen gave me this coat and hat personally and I will not take it off until the day I die' he says. We all call him Bean. Cus of the beanie hat. Nobody actually knows his name.

Whenever I pass him I ask how he is. He asks me about school. I tell him it's shit. He tells me *'stick with it kid.'* Then I pop into Tescos and ask if he wants anythin'. He always asks for a cheese sandwich cuz he's a vegetarian. *'No meat has passed these lips in sixty years'.*

We've got it down to a science now. I take one sandwich. He takes the other. And we just chat. He listens to anythin' I say, gobbles up my words like Alphabetti Spaghetti. It used to be the best part of my day chattin' to Bean. I miss it.

One day. I'm with my mate Connor. He's just moved schools. Propa tiny he is. But you don't call him tiny. Propa spotty he is. But you don't call him spotty. You don't dare call him anythin'. Because that is Connor. But when you are with Connor, you are someone. The birds shit on you less.

We pass Bean. I'm thinkin' not today Bean. Bean doesn't clock this. *'Hey kid! How was school!?'*
Shit. Connor looks down from his BMX. *'He your boyfriend?'*
'Nah'
An' I just run into Tescos and Bean calls back *'Bring us back a sandwich will ya kid, remember, no meat has passed these lips in sixty years'*
Connor smiles. A sickly smile. Makes my guts shake.

I pick up two Lucozades cuz it's two for one. And Connor picks up a chicken sandwich. And we are back outside and I'm thinkin' great, this is just goin' to end. We're going to get on our bikes and ride them streets.

Then it happens.

Connor spits *'Oi'*. Looks at Bean in his warm welcomin' eyes. And says, *'I bought you a chicken sandwich mate'*. Bean like the gentleman he is says, *'Thank you, young man, but I don't eat meat.'*

Connor grips the sandwich tighta. *'Tesco's finest mate. Proper expensive shit, you not goin' to eat it?'*

And suddenly, Connor starts rubbin' the sandwich over Bean's face. Smearin' it and smearin' it. Bean could easily take Connor, he's twice the size of him but he just sits there! Doesn't move or say a thing. He just stares at me!

And this makes Connor angrier. So he grabs Bean's nose tight. Bean is forced to open his mouth and in the chicken goes. Chunks and chunks of chicken! Dribblin' back out and getting shoved back in! Mayo dribblin' over Bean's coat. His amazin' coat. The coat the Queen gave him!

I wanna say, *'Stop Connor, he's a cool guy'*. But I don't. I just stand there. Trying to telepathically communicate how sorry I am to Bean. Cuz when you are with Connor you are someone!

Connor gets bored cuz Bean doesn't react. Connor doesn't even look at him again. We just get back on our bikes and ride them streets.

I see him in the distance. Sweatin' in his now stained coat. Spitting out processed chicken. I'll never forget that image.

The next day I go back there early to catch him before school. He's there. I say, *'Cheese sandwich Bean?'*

He looks at me for a while.

'I'm not hungry today kid. I'm not very hungry.'

'My Mum would not have seen my Dad like that'

Edward Sayeed

> **A young mixed-race man has to decide whether he wants to date a woman who likes him because he's black. For ages 18 and above.**

The thing is, like...that's not me. Other guys, they can play that game. I'm not gonna tell them they can't. But me...when someone says that to *me*...

I don't reckon, honestly, like really, that that's what happened with my mum... I mean I know, obviously I don't wanna see her like that, so you're gonna tell me I'm not actually looking at it, like it is. But *my mum*...

No.

So when this girl goes and says it... I mean I do like her, I'm not gonna lie, I could see myself...and her. Definitely. *Definitely*... And we were getting on nicely. I say, 'You wanna meet some time?', she said 'Yeah', it was all natural. There was no...doubt, but no weirdness either. We weren't like staring at each other, like I just wanna... get you in bed, you know...obviously we do want that, but there was more, there was much more, like there has to be, if it's gonna be some proper thing. And I was all... *I was actually* thinking about Mum. How I'd be telling her about this girl and all the stuff we done together, cos she's always going on at me, Mum, about this girlfriend, that girlfriend, why'd you always pick ones like that? And I'm looking at this girl, and I'm thinking, yeah... Mum's not gonna want me to split with *her*. Even the little talk, you know. The *small* talk. I mean I always thought small talk was bullshit. But she's shown me, just in this five minutes. I've seen that small talk. Is a big, big thing. And it's fun man...with a girl like that. You get her, she gets you... And then she says it...

Pause.

Like I say, other guys... I know guys if I told them, they'd be all like, 'What's the matter with you? She's put it on a plate for you.' But that's the problem. That's *exactly*[1] the problem.

'I always thought I'd end up with a black guy.'

I'm, I'm not *a black guy... I'm me.* And I could see after she said it, that she never meant to. It's cos we was speaking natural, words was flowing out. But that just killed it. She started tryna say something, but she was all nervous, she couldn't say it right. I finished my drink, said goodbye, and I left.

Pause.

But I didn't delete her number...yet.

I mean maybe she *knew*...like sometimes women *know*, don't they? Like maybe one of the things she knew about the guy she was gonna be with was that he was black or like me, like half-black. And it came out in the wrong way. At the wrong time.

But why'd she say that one thing? She could say anything. A five foot eleven guy. A guy who's four years older than her. That supports the same team as her. Where's that come from that she's gone and said *that?*

And I keep thinking...that my Mum...would not have seen my Dad like that.

But boy she's...and I just know Mum'd love her.

Nashville

Rabiah Hussain

> **A British Indian woman auditions for a country music TV competition. Age stated in monologue as 24 years old.**

NIKITA, 24, young British Indian girl. Walks onto stage wearing a long dark jacket and carrying a laptop bag – very corporate.

Yes, I'm ready... Where?... Here?... OK... Sure, sure. How many before me? Three? OK. Great. Would it be OK if I just practiced a little? Great, thanks.

> *She straightens up. A pause before she breaks out into Dolly Parton's '9 to 5'.*

You'll tell me when it's time, right? Thanks... I'm quite nervous. Really nervous, actually. Are the others good? Of course, they are. It can't be easy to win a trip to Nashville.

> *She takes off her jacket to reveal brightly coloured clothes on underneath. She fixes her clothes and hair.*

Where am I from? Hounslow... Really from?... Um. Hounslow East... Yeah, guess my accent is pretty good.

> *Pause.*

Two now? OK. OK... No, there's no one here with me. I left work early and came straight here. Told them I had a dentist appointment. I can't tell a group of financial advisers that I'm off to audition for the country music version of *The X Factor*. They don't even know I like country music! They don't know much about me. I have a picture of Dottie West on my desk. But no one has ever asked me about it. I think they only see me as...well, who I am at work. I've never quite figured out if that's the right version of me. Do you know what I mean?

    Pause.

You didn't think Indians were into country music? Well. I don't think many English people are either, are they? But my dad never went a single day without listening to Kenny Rogers. He would fall asleep and wake up listening to him. My brothers hated it. And Mum developed some sort of audio forcefield to tune it all out. But I loved it.

    Pause.

Do they know? No, I didn't tell them either. They don't really see me in that way. They don't...know me. Not really. They know I love country music though. I have posters up in my bedroom of all the country stars you can think of. And stacks of CDs. Some are my dad's. But he's never really asked me either. I don't know. Maybe I am some version of me that everyone else knows but I don't. Does that make sense? But I'd love to see the look on everyone's faces if I win. I think I'll tell them only then. Not before.

One? So, I'm on after?

She continues to sing '9 to 5' as she puts on large earrings. She stops singing abruptly.

I don't think can I do this. No, really. I mean, who am I kidding?... I'm never going to win. If I lose... I'm going to turn around and go back to Hounslow. Back to my desk and my bedroom. Back to normal life. The places where I know who I am. I'm sorry about this. I'm sorry. I just can't.

She picks up her stuff and almost runs offstage.

She stops and turns around and walks back.

Seems determined to carry on.

Sometimes, letting others decide who are you seems easier than finding out for yourself. It's going to be scary. But I need to know... Yes, I'm ready. Three, two, one... Let's go.

She steps forward.

Naughty Boy

Femi Keeling

> **Teacher by day, sex phone operator by night, with the two worlds often merging. For ages 18 and above.**

(To audience.) It's definitely him. I know his voice. He's got a lisp that he is desperately trying to hide, and he is failing.

(On the phone, in a voice that does not sound like her own.) Take off all your clothes and sit on the cold, hard floor.

(To audience.) The good thing about having a performing arts degree is that unlike most sex-line hosts, I know how to act. The funny thing about this call in particular is that he pays me for my expertise Monday to Friday, but he's got no idea he's paying me for it now.

(On the phone.) Did I give you permission to speak? Then shut your dirty little mouth.

(To audience.) The other teachers say it's bad luck I joined the school this year. That it's unfortunate that my first job out of teacher training is in a school where the head is a bully. Word around the school is that his wife left him for another woman three years ago and since then he treats all the women teachers like shit. Like he wants to make us pay for what she did.

*(On the phone.) Tell me that you've been a naughty boy!
You know what we do with naughty boys, don't you?*

(To audience.) You're right. It is interesting that I allow
myself to be bullied during the day when I talk to
men like this at night, but I like to keep my two jobs
separate. At school I am hard-working and very quiet.
Respectable. Respectful. And last week, when I sat
down in his office for our meeting I also focused on
being polite. Gracious. Graceful. I began to carefully lay
out my ideas on improvements for the drama course but
he shut me down before I could finish my first thought.
(With heavy lisp.) 'It's my school, Patrice,' he said, 'I don't
take suggestions.'

*(On the phone.) I'm spanking you now. Your left cheek is
on fire and I'm still spanking you. Beg me to stop.*

(To audience.) Mrs Francis is taking early retirement at
the end of this year. She's given up trying to get through
to him. Miss Scope has been on leave for the past two
months due to stress. She has a panic attack every time
she sees him. And every break time, since I joined the
school, we all sit around talking about him. We should
be talking about the kids, talking about *Eastenders*,
but instead we're consoling each other, sharing coping
strategies, looking for job opportunities. It's like we're in
an abusive relationship.

*(On the phone.) I want you to listen and repeat after me,
OK? I want you to say everything I say, word for word. If
you miss a word – if you stutter, or stumble – I'm gonna
make you pay, OK?*

(To audience.) Of course nobody wanted to do it. I suggested it and we all agreed that one of us would arrange a meeting with him and then we'd all turn up, but nobody wanted to be the one to arrange the meeting. Then Miss Manning put my name forward and before I knew it they'd all agreed. He'd be happy to meet with me, you see, because I'm so young, and quiet. I scheduled a meeting for tomorrow and I assured them all that I'd find the right words to let him know that we're not going to stand for it anymore. But I lied to them. I couldn't think. I couldn't think of what I could possibly say to this man, this bully, who doesn't take suggestions and probably wouldn't let me finish. How would I get him to listen?

(On the phone.) Are you ready, naughty boy? (In her normal voice.) Then say, 'Hi Patrice.' Say, 'I can't wait for our meeting tomorrow; I can't wait to listen to your suggestions and give you everything you want.'

Nithan

Mahad Ali

A school caretaker gets fired for spreading his Scientologist views on the students, so he exacts revenge on the whole school. For ages 18 and above.

So there I was going about my usual business, you know cleaning, fixing a broken fence, mending a leaking pipe. Helping because that's what I like to do, help people. When he just came out of nowhere and tapped me on the shoulder. I turned around and I just saw him walking away.

My office now! He shouts.

I don't do confrontation, maybe he knows this and that's why he felt he can so easily try to publicly humiliate me like that.

So we get into his office and he lays down the law.

'As you know at St Xavier while we may be a Church of England School, we have an inclusive approach when it comes to other faiths and cultures, we are a rather forward-thinking school but...well...we draw the line at proselytising.'

Prezslo...what? I say.

'In short trying to convert others to your religion, it goes against the social, moral and spiritual character of our school.'

He produced a piece of literature and slammed it on the table.

'I had a parent complaining about this! You know what she called it "Sci-fi, pseudo–Christian, poppy cock". This is simply unacceptable in an age of radicalisation and Islamic extremism!'

Radicalisation! Extremism! I'm a Scientologist!

'At work you're a caretaker, you shouldn't be speaking to about such matters, bearing this in mind we have little choice but to suspend you...'

My head is spinning. What? Why? How? I wasn't trying to convert anyone... I was volunteering, starting the karate club to teach kids self-defence because when I was growing up no one taught me how to stand up for myself and I got bullied. But when the kids started... well we got talking and you know at that age you're intellectually curious... Like who are we? Why are we here? What is our purpose?

I thought I had the answers, well not the answers... I was just trying to answer their questions. Again I was trying to help and I thought the karate training would help heighten their spiritual awareness. But like sometimes trying to help can get you into trouble, like giving advice that is unwanted or breaking up a drunken fight. But he didn't have to embarrass me the way he did.

MAHAD ALI

Suspending me wasn't right! But revenge is a dish best served cold and yeah I don't believe in revenge but he had it coming! So I went to the press...if they are going to call me a crazy scientologist I might as well act like one! I can't wait to see his face when he sees tomorrows headline in the local Gazette. 'Scientologist infiltrates local school'... Ofsted are going to have a field day with him!

No Thigh Gaps Allowed

Titilola Dawudu

> **A dancer who does not have the traditional dancer body, is ready to give up and start a revolution... until she gets a callback. For ages 16 and above.**

Well that was a waste of time! Why do I bother? Why? Why? Because I actually think I'm a good – no, great – dancer. I'm definitely better then some of those skinny cows with their wide thigh gaps.

I'm so annoyed at myself – I'm drenched in sweat *and* I danced on a dodgy ankle. Ah thanks Mel – that would be great. But please rub gently. I really need to ice it. Hang on – let me sit down. *(Sits on the floor and takes off dance shoe.)*

I know I'm meant to be giving you advice and passing on my dancer-knowledge – but I just don't know what to tell you. It seems like a repeat pattern. I go to these auditions, I get scrutinised – and I know the other girls don't get it as much. It's my bum and thighs – it's becoming more and more apparent that I'm not dancer material. I'm always giving correct alignment, my arch is strong and *I'm* strong. That's my thing – I always get told I'm strong. Sometimes the strongest they've seen and graceful – but it never comes together. I never get a callback and I know it's because I don't look the part that they've envisioned for the piece.

I wish I could tell you to hang on in there – that sometimes it's hard, but it's worth it. But more and more I just want to scream and tell these emaciated-stuck-in-the-past, living-life-vicariously-through-whoever-their-next-ingénue-slash-muse-is – choreographers that they've got it all wrong. They're not looking at the bigger picture. And telling me my attitude's not right because I speak up and want feedback as to why I didn't get the audition. Well how do I learn? I don't want this to be some sad story of a dancer whose parents didn't understand her love for it, never went to see her dance and she failed anyway.

Can you do the other ankle as well? I'm just so tense. Melanie – I know I said I'd help you, but after that audition – I just feel deflated. No – no, actually mad. I'm mad. Pissed off that I have to deal with this same old, same old shit. Because I don't look the part. I'm not getting it. Getting what? What am I not getting?

You know what Mel – I can't keep doing this. I need to change it. You know – it? 'It' is all of this. I need to change all of this: how I'm being made to feel, not getting anywhere. I need to make more of a noise somehow. You know – like take it to the Culture secretary. Write to someone important in government. Do a Ted Talk. Start my own – yes, start my own dance school. Embrace all the dancers who look like me – no thigh gaps allowed! That's my story. That's who I am, Melanie. And you can be a part of it – you can help me raise the voice of the voiceless in dance. It'll be great. It's empowering. Don't most successful stories start with some type of sob story? Some hill someone had to climb? A conversation outside of a crappy audition lead to an idea, which lead to a dance school, which lead to lives being changed! No more waste of time auditions for me!

Sees that she has a text message.

Oh – I – I got it. I actually got it... I can't believe –

Erm...yeah, so Melanie, look, sometimes it's up and down. Good days, bad days, you know? *(Packs up her bag and puts back on her shoe.)* You've got to take it for what it's for. It's meant to toughen you up for the big wide world.

Thanks, my ankle's OK now.

Nobody's Nose

Ayesha Manazir Siddiqi

> **A woman wants a nose job but decides against it when she realises she'd be erasing who she is. Age stated in monologue as 28 years old.**

REGINA, female, Caribbean, 28.

Wow. Seriously? That's what it'll look like, huh?
Wow.
Wow.

You know when I was younger, I used to pinch my nose, like this, all the time. I'd hold it like that even while I slept. Then, I'd check in the morning to see if it had become thinner. Hah.

No I had, I'd thought about it many times before. As a teenager especially. People teased me sometimes, they said, oh too bad you don't have a nose like your sister's, that would have been so much prettier. My sister has my dad's nose, you see. So, yeah.

Payment plan? Yeah. I can pay upfront. I'm using my mum's inheritance. I feel like she would have wanted me to. She always said, you have to listen to your heart, Regina. I guess this is doing that, right?

Although when I used to tell her I wanted a nose job, as a teenager, she would say, Regina, what do you want a

white girl's nose for? I would get so mad when she said
that. I don't want a white girl's nose. It's not like that.
But you know, even if I did, which I don't, how is it my
fault? Like, why are we always picking on people like,
Michael Jackson and Lil' Kim for changing their faces
instead of the racist dickheads that made them do it –
sorry. I just mean we shouldn't be criticizing those guys.
They're survivors, those guys, just trying to live, that's
all. I mean, I'm sure you know, right? To be where you
are, such a great doctor, as a person of colour...

You don't identify as a person of colour?
Oh. Sorry.
What do you identify as then?
'Just a human being.'
Oh. OK. Right.

Do you think, doctor. I mean. I don't know. Do you think
that's what I'm trying to do by changing this? To become
more like, 'just a human being'?

No, sorry. I don't know what I mean either.
Yes. Yes, I do understand the consultation's only free
if I go ahead with the procedure.

It's just – the more I look at that photo, that photo of me
in a few weeks' time. The more it looks like I'm rubbing
my mother off of my face, you know? I mean. That nose.
It's nobody's nose, you know? Nobody's nose.

Off The Streets

Naomi Joseph

> **A homeless young boy is being questioned about a break-in. Age stated in monologue as 15 years old.**

RICKY. Male, fifteen, baby-faced and petite.

A police station. RICKY is being interviewed.

Don't I get a phone call or something?

Nah...doesn't matter. I don't have anyone to...

Look there's a difference between breaking and entering and just...entering. Right? She...she normally leaves the window open and I mean like *wide* open. You can hear the TV from the street! And she usually leaves her cup of tea on the ledge – you know how careful I have to be not to trip over it when I'm climbing in?

No. I don't go back to the same place too often... Dunno... Don't want to ruin a good thing I guess. Look I know what I'm doing is wrong... Coz there's nowhere else for me to go!... Hostels? Yeah right, full of smackheads, crackheads and pissheads – no thanks... Nah no way. Can you imagine sleeping on cardboard pillows and wearing bin-liner ponchos? I can't hack that life.

...Yeah... Nah I don't know her. Never met her. Staked it out for ages. Saw she never closes that window and...

bingo! Free Airbnb... On the sofa... Deep sleeper I guess... Yeah...cos it feels like...for a split second it feels normal. Like living at my nanna's again. Soft carpet under my feet. Smell of burnt toast and hot tea. It's warm...it's...it's nice. Not like the places they put me in after nanna... Worse than being on the streets.

I don't take liberties if that's what you mean! Nah never. OK yeah when you put it like that...*maybe* like leftovers she threw in the bin yeah but not like *food* food.

Look, that night I was desperate. Everywhere was closing and this man...when you look like me you're easy prey on the streets, know what I mean? I legged it to the block of flats. I look up and for the first time ever it wasn't open. I had to do something! I couldn't risk... So I grabbed a brick. I didn't know she was behind the curtain. Is she OK? I didn't mean to...what's gonna happen to me?

One Day, One Act

Unique Spencer

> **A woman is betrayed by her husband and stands up in court to set the truth free. For ages 30 and above.**

CLAIRE stands in a courtroom, dressed in her army uniform. She has a glass of water in her hand which she holds with both hands.

Your honour I'm here today representing myself because I have to set the truth free.

See takes a sip of water and composes herself.

I loved my husband so very much. We had been married thirteen years. We started our careers together in the army. We were happy but we wasn't complete.

CLAIRE sips some water slowly and calmly.

A day before he came home a card came through the letterbox. I had decided to do something special for his birthday. Everyone was having a great time, I baked my famous strawberry cheesecake and homemade burgers. All his favorites. We sang happy birthday and he opened his gifts. Just as he's opening his last gift I remember the card he got in the post. He opens it and a picture of a baby falls out and it wasn't a picture of him as a child so I just thought it's an inside joke with a friend.

That night I was in bed and I heard the front door shut, as I looked for my husband he wasn't there. I got up and I went to the window and I saw him sitting in a car with a lady and a child. They were arguing and then she got out of the car and went to the boot and it's full with luggage. He goes to the back of the car and kisses the child and says something to her which calms her down. She got back in the car and drove away.

My husband came back in to our house, back in to our bed, and thought I was asleep and that I would never know that he...he...he...betrayed me.

So yes on that one day I committed one act that I will now live with for the rest of my life, but at least, your honour, I will sleep with the truth.

Party Animal

Bushra Laskar

> **A party planner is questioned by the police about a missing pony. Age stated in monologue as 30 years old.**

Early evening, police station. SAIMA, thirty, is dressed in a smart knee-length bodycon dress.

OK, maybe I shouldn't have hired that pony for the party, but the client gets what the client wants especially if she's putting down that kind of money.

And no, I'm not saying her spoilt little brat deserved to get kicked in the face by a pony high on birthday cake, but I'm also not saying I didn't laugh when he did. You can't arrest me for that, officer. The kid was fine, you saw him. A bit of concussion never hurt anyone. Poor horse was scared out of his wits though – the disco lights, the people. His handler was at the bar doing shots with the birthday boy's dad, did he tell you that? He's the one you should be questioning, not me. How the hell would I know where the pony's run off to? I'm a party planner, not a horse whisperer.

Please, officer, I take my job very seriously. I'm good at what I do and I've built up quite a reputation in my field which I'm not about to throw away by stealing a prize-winning pony.

Sometimes things just get out of hand, you know what it's like. Drunken, loud dads in designer suits. Screeching women struggling to dance in sky-high heels. Ugh. I bet a number of my guests end up getting arrested by you later for being drunk and disorderly. And I can imagine that's not your favourite part of the job but you take pride in your work, just like me. I can see it; your desk's neatly organised, your uniform's on point, but there's something, something niggling in the back of your mind, right? I get it – you've learnt your craft, you've worked your way up and now you're here and you're thinking to yourself, why aren't I happy? What is it about this job that's just not sitting well with me?

I mean, I give people what they want. I humour every strange and elaborate request, I take all the stress away from their special occasions so they can just relax and have a great time, and I do it all without going over budget. I make people happy! But maybe I don't want to make people happy. Maybe I don't want to make their special occasions special. Maybe I just want to run away from everyone and live in a cottage in the woods with just a labradoodle and my Whitney Houston albums, cos honestly, people just get on my tits. Why should I make other people happy if I literally can't stand any of them?

Beat.

Honestly officer, if I knew what had happened to the pony I'd tell you. He was the only guest there I actually liked. He was gorgeous, wasn't he? Lovely mane.

Rani's Revenge

Paula David

> **A woman bitter about her father's other family, tells him she is to marry her half-brother. Age stated in monologue as 21 years old.**

I can hear you breathing. I know you're still there.

This is ironic. As a child in boarding school I was desperate for you to come get me. I counted every day to the holidays, imagining that big hug I would get because you missed your little princess. I felt so completely desperate when you didn't arrive knowing I would travel alone to Grandma's.

All those times you didn't turn up, you were with Divit weren't you? It all makes sense, the festivals you missed. It was always just Grandma and me, while you were with you new wife and son Divit in Scotland. Does Grandma know about your lifelong deceit? Is this why you were never with me when I visited her? Is Divit why I never saw your parents. Why couldn't I go with you when you remarried, how could you abandon me daddy Why?

Well, what if I told you that it's too late for the truth. What if I told you Divit and I have already spoken of marriage. All the suitors you sent to me over the last two years were just like you selfish, self-serving, expecting a woman to be seen and not heard. Well Divit isn't like that, he is a strong man with ambition and needs a strong woman by his side. He told me, I am that woman. How do you feel about your precious son now that he has asked his sister to marry him?

I want to believe you were waiting for the right moment to tell your new wife about me. But you had twenty one years daddy, maybe you just didn't love me enough.

It's just like you to believe I did this to spite you or to get revenge. You really believe the world revolves around you.

Our love is real daddy.

Revenge? No, this is the justice I deserve.

Rekha

Safaa Benson-Effiom

> **A woman is telling a father that she is in love with his daughter. Age implied in monologue as 40 years old.**

It didn't start out like this. I don't think it was either of our intentions to fall in love.

But then, does anyone ever *intend* to fall in love? I don't think so. It's something that just happens to you.

You're taken along for a ride, no idea when it'll end but hoping to God it never does.

I didn't plan to fall in love with your daughter.
I didn't know that was something I was capable of, something I was mentally or emotionally able to do: fall in love with somebody's *DAUGHTER*!

It's new. In every sense of the word. And not just for me, for her as well!
And you know, anytime I pause to really think about it, it actually makes me laugh. I thought I was too old for new things. And yet here I am, basking in the glow of a new love.

For the first time in fifteen years, I'm happy. For the first time in fifteen years, I'm not alone. For the first time in fifteen years, I have someone in my life who cares about me, truly cares about me: who worries about whether or not I've eaten, who asks about my day and actually wants to know about it, who senses when I'm lost and helps bring me back.

And that someone – that kind, sweet, perfect, generous, loving person is at home, crying, devastated by her mother's threat to disown her.

Please. Help me understand. Because for the life of me, I cannot understand why she should suffer for being happy.

Why?
Is it still honour over happiness? Even now?

> *Beat.*
>
> *Beat.*
>
> *Beat.*

I didn't plan to fall in love with your daughter. But sometimes your soul senses something in another person and reaches out for it. Before there was love, our souls recognised something in each others. A hidden pain. A pain not easily noticed by anyone who hasn't experienced that particular pain. Do you understand how elusive, how rare that is?

My sister died when she was twenty-five. When I was twenty-five.

We weren't – um, I don't know the science – we weren't identical. But still, when I was twenty-five, I lost my other half. So imagine my surprise when I met your daughter. Like me: a former one of two, half of a whole. How does that happen? Seven billion people on earth and your daughter walks into my book club!

I never even imagined there could be anyone out there who knew what this was like. What it was like to go through life with that constant sense of something being missing, constantly feeling like you're going to fall because that crucial thing that keeps you upright isn't there.

At least when you lose a parent, a friend, a child, there is help out there. As sad as it is, you know there is someone else out there who feels that pain, who gets it. But there is no support group for the twin left behind. You were formed together, grew together, walked through life together.

I never dreamt I could find someone who would really and truly feel my pain. And in doing so, really and truly bring me joy, a feeling I never thought I'd get to experience ever again.

I thought that maybe God had decided my life was to be an unhappy one. I forgot that God doesn't work like that.

For her. Please. Reconsider.

Running Out of Time
Bisola Elizabeth Alabi

> **A man owes a large amount of money and he fears for his life. Age stated in monologue as 26 years old.**

AVINASH PATEL, known as Avi (26 years old, Scottish) is talking to his cousin Taahira.

Listen, the reason I've asked you to be here is I have no one else to turn to...umm I don't know how to say this but I have less than two minutes to live.

Beat.

Can you lend me some money? I owe a tiny bit of money to some very charming people, who have requested they'd like to have it back within the next two minutes...plus interest. But I swear on my parents' lives I will pay you back. It's just a little bit of cash you won't miss it for too long.

I know I have the worst track record for keeping my promises but I promise you this time round it's different.

Drops the façade.

Well, I owe them *(muffled)* £25k. I said I owe them £25k!

Beat.

I need you to give me...I mean lend me £25k.

It's not funny Taahira. No, no, no please *dinnae* (don't) go. I'm deadly serious I need you. This isn't a prank I'm really desperate, look at me! Have you ever seen me likes this? Listen, I owe a lot of money to some very scary people and if I don't pay them back within the next two minutes, well ONE minute now, you might as well call me dog's dinner.

Oh God! I think I can hear footsteps outside. You're the only person that I have. When we were kids it was always you who had my back. I *dinnae* (don't) want to die. Please *dinnae* (don't) let me die.

Do you think I'm proud of this? Do you think I'm proud that I have to beg you for money? I don't want to be like this anymore, I can see my life flash before my eyes and I realise I'm a fucking asshole but like I said you're all I've got in this world.

They're here.

   Beat.

I know I can't run and I know I can't hide so I might as well just face the music. But you're here as well. Do you honestly think they will let you go if you're a witness? So you have a choice either give me the money or... Well you'll see for yourself what they'll do to *us*.

Sabina the Superhero
Paula David

> **A woman can't bear to see her ailing mother suffer, so she takes matters into her own hands. For ages 18 and above.**

I've put your crossword puzzle in your sewing box, so you'll be able to find it tomorrow mum. That's right, you get some sleep. The doctor says rest is important. You'll be less anxious and confused tomorrow if you get plenty of rest. Thank goodness for these sleeping pills. You're getting so much better at taking them mum.

Do you remember the stories you used to tell me, when you put me to bed? Fairy stories. Raziya was always my favourite. She had special powers. The first was to see the soul's desire and the second, to detect a lie and the truth behind it. I used to pretend I had the power to move things with my mind, Do you remember? You used to humour me by pretending I'd moved your arm or your leg. I was ten years old before you stopped playing that game. I miss you mum.

Woah, mum you're OK, you're OK, you just need to hold still. It's gonna pass, please don't scream mum, it's gonna be OK, it won't last long just hold on.

There you are, I said it wouldn't last long. Please don't cry. I can't bare to see you cry.

It's just one of those mini strokes, remember I explained it yesterday. That's it just lay back, breath, that's better.

Have some more sleeping pills, that'll calm you down. That's it, drink it slowly. Is that enough water? There you go.

Is it cruel to imagine you drifting into a peaceful sleep that goes on and on...and... There would be no more mini strokes, no more uncontrollable crying, or angry outbursts. I'm still nursing that bruise above my eye from Friday. I know you want to join Dad.

Have a few more pills, you'll sleep better, just sit up a little more, that's it swallow, a few more sips. There you go lay back down.

I know you're in there somewhere. I know you still exist. But you're shrinking . Every day the cruel monstrosity of dementia grows stronger and you get weaker.

Maybe these sleeping pills will quieten the monster and allow my beautiful mum a few moments with me.

Here you are mum. Just take a few more, maybe four this time, open up, that's it, swallow, a bit more water?

You see, you look a little more peaceful already. I miss the calm mum. I miss sitting with a cup tea and fruit cake and laughing about how shit my boss is or how bad Paul is at buying birthday presents. Do remember how long we laughed when he bought a bike for himself for my birthday. So we could go on bike rides together, he said. He was so pleased with himself. *(She laughs.)* If you could hear me mum we'd be laughing together.

Take some more pills mum. You'll be more relaxed. Here we go, that's right everything will be much better after you've taken all of these pills.

It's kindness that makes me want to stop you're suffering. You will drift off now to a place where your daughter doesn't put you on the toilet, feed you knowing you'll bring up your food, watch you lash out when you're confused and in pain during one of your mini strokes. You'll be with Dad again, you'll be happy again. Maybe I have special powers after all. When the morning comes I will have made all your pain and distress go away.

Sarah

Mahad Ali

> **A woman has to tell one of her employees that he is fired. And the employee is her husband. For ages 25 and above.**

SARAH gets up from her seat and is clearly animated.

When we were in law school you were always telling me that I didn't have what it takes to get to the top. That to be number one I had to be ruthless, a killer – be willing to feed the sheep to the wolves!

Beat.

Yes you did! But I wasn't raised that the way. Anyway, Nanny used to tell me and yes I know you don't care about Nanny but I do! She used to say...

Beat.

No...can you let me finish...she used to say...
'When you're at work you have to treat people with respect. Stand up straight, have confidence, never dress sloppy as it conveys laziness, speak correctly but softly, loudness portrays aggression – maintain your strength while exhibiting patience with others.'

And I don't care if you think she is old, she is wise! And her advice has taken me far.

So that's why I took you on Jamie as my assistant.

I know you didn't ask but I wanted to show you things can be done another way... But then I noticed things at work, things started going badly – the staff questioning every decision I made, the whispering in corners, meetings without me... I tried to be calm about it but...

SARAH holds up the newspaper.

But then it got into the papers...look – 'it's only sensible that the business employs people of the highest calibre and those who have a track record of success in their respective fields.'

Track record! I'm the senior partner at a law firm, if that's not success...

SARAH breathes a deep breath.

It continues 'she has got this wrong from the beginning. It is an inbuilt arrogance. She appoints mates, people who don't have the relevant experience'.

That's when I realised Jamie...things had started going wrong, when you arrived. Why are you rolling your eyes like that! I wasn't born yesterday.

SARAH has her arms folder in anger.

What'd you mean 'you've got to show them whose boss? Lay down the law!' That's not your place!

I don't care if you're my husband...this is work and my business. If I cut you off chances are you handed me the scissors.

What'd you mean, what am I talking about?

You're fired!

Saved

Karim Khan

Saving the life of a little boy brings back memories for a woman whose younger brother drowned years before. For ages 18 and above.

Your door was open, I should'a knocked but. *(To herself.)* Shit, sorry I shouldn't've come.

I caught the first train I could from Marylebone and legged it here. Hear me out please mum, I know it's weird, me here after so long... I've got these butterflies, that icky...sickiness. I just needed to share it with you – I saved a little boy's life. *(Pause).* Look at me mum – I finished work, and I was walking down the street and I saw him lying on the floor. Mum? Loads of people were round him, no one knew what to do. I went to him, and performed CPR. I was dead nervous thought I'd get somat wrong, make him worse, God could you imagine, but there weren't any paramedics or ambulance, and I did first aid at work so I thought fuck it *sorry*. But it saved him, that's was the paramedic said. *(Louder.)* She said, are you listening mum? She said to me: you saved this little boy's life. His name was Ali, Ali Shafiq and he was about to die on me mum, unconscious, I thought it was happenin' all over again. But I saved. Him. Seven years old, his mum said. I spoke to her later. He was this tall, just about here. You still got that height board you measured us on? I think it was the same as...his, give or take a few inches, almost identical I swear, you know mum I felt somethin' today, I felt him here, I felt he was watching over me and spurrin' me on. Sounds dumb don't it? Like, it felt like he lifted this weight off me and he was talking to me,

'I forgive you Reena, now you have to forgive yourself' but I can't forgive myself can I?

Where you going mum? Sit down please – talk to me. Did you get it? – the letter I sent you. It was s'posed to be truthful – heartfelt – bet you binned it as soon as you saw my shitty writing. 'It's the girl that killed my son', not your daughter, not the one that tried to save him from drowning, but couldn't cos she was only small and scared. It was an accident, and I'm sorry, sorry that it was my idea and I couldn't do...anything to save him, but I loved him too. I miss him too. I don't need you to forgive me if you don't want to. *(Sharp intake of breath.)*

Cos I think I've finally, finally forgiven *[myself]*.

This was a bad idea, I shouldn't have come, I'm sorry I disturbed you.

'Seriously, it was unreal'

Edward Sayeed

> **A young woman settles with her life being about pasties and meat pies, while all her friends are moving on and going to university. For ages 18 and above.**

Seriously, it was unreal. All these guys. 'Let me give you my number, maybe we can hook up later.' You let Clem choose what you're gonna wear, do your make up, you become like some...magnet. It was a good night. Really good. We had some jokes, had some drinks. I've gotta choose which guys I'm gonna call. I wish Clem was here to talk about them. I guess I'll see her in her uni holidays... although she'll probably go back to her parents mainly.

Like that's what happened with Jess... Jess comes sometimes, she come at New Year's, but...she's changed, man. She called me when she got there, 'Oh yeah, freshers week and all that'. But when she told me about it and then I said, I don't know what, nothing crazy, just like 'Oh yeah, babe, that sounds good', just something like that, she went... I swear she went all *cold*. And we finished talking and whatever, and then a few texts. Then nothing. Like I'd been really rude. And I wasn't, I properly wasn't... Alright *maybe*. *Maybe* I sounded a bit *bored*. Maybe I seen enough of all her updates, 'Uni, uni, uni'. I reckon I could draw you a plan, of every fucking thing that happened at her freshers' week. So if I was like not completely, *(affected happiness)* 'Oh my God, that's so great', you can see why, innit?

Anyway, I'd much rather have a night out round here, like with Clem last Friday. I tried to get her to stay for next weekend, but she said she had to get up to halls.

It's funny how me and Clem's been tight this last year. I never knew her so much before with me and Jess being the year above her at college. But Clem and me's had some mad fun man. Every shift I'd be looking to see if we was on the rota together. We'd be laughing about some of the customers, thinking what we was gonna do that evening...now it's like... I never felt before how heavy all them pastry trays and that are, putting them in and out the oven all day. You feel tired, man, after ten hours, I'm telling you... I texted that to Clem. She must've been busy with freshers' week, that's probably why she never texted back. That girl *knows* how to enjoy herself.

There was just one thing, before she went, I didn't like. She went, 'Weren't you in Mr Daniels' class for upper sixth?' I said, 'Yeah'. And she went 'Oh... I thought everyone in Mr Daniels' class got good grades.'

What's she saying that for? I wasn't trying for good grades, I was chilling with Jess...

    Short pause.

I said to Mr Daniels when we got our results, I said, 'I'm gonna retake 'em, Sir.' He said, 'You can if you want...but if I was you I wouldn't bother.'

    Short pause.

(Kisses her teeth leading immediately into saying.)
Whatever man, I don't wanna go on no freshers' week...
I hate even hearing about them.

201

Sheen

Safaa Benson-Effiom

> **A woman has a secret she is telling an ex-boyfriend. For ages 18 and above.**

I've spent the last six years thinking about this exact moment. Attempting to craft the perfect first meeting. Daydreaming. Play acting.
Wondering what you'd think. And then what you'd say.
Just...imagining how it would be. How we would be.

I've spent the last six years wondering what it would be like to be with you. Again.

But I didn't plan for this.

It feels like the entire world has fallen away and this Us. Here. Together. Is all that's left.
I asked you here to tell you one thing. But now. Now that you're right here...

She begins to reach a hand across the table.

Now all I want to tell you is how much I...

She snatches her hand back, reacting to him withdrawing his own. She smiles to herself. Beat.

I know you want to know what it is. My huge black hole of a secret.

Beat.

That dark cloud that hung over our entire relationship. And the truth is: I always wanted to tell you.

Honestly, every single time your eyes met mine I had to bite my tongue to stop the words from falling from my mouth.

And you knowing – even though you didn't know what it was, just the fact that you knew there was something

That was hard.

I started seeing someone.

To talk to.

But only recently.

I make a four hour round trip once a week. Further away than I need to go.

Far enough away that I don't have to worry, don't really have to worry about anything getting back to anyone.

So I did. Session number one. Minutes in. I hadn't even said hello or introduced myself and this person, this total stranger

I told her.

And again, so many ways I expected it to go, so many ways I expected her to react, things I expected her to do, to say...

She barely bat an eyelid! For a second, I thought she hadn't heard me.

Maybe she was expecting something else, something bigger, something shocking.

... I thought it was shocking!

I guess all these comic book movies have desensitised everyone to this stuff.

> *She looks at him, giving that last thought time to land. Nothing.*

> *Beat.*

Hmmm.
And her complete lack of a reaction got me thinking.
If I'd only just trusted you back then, maybe none of this...

Would it make a difference? Now? If I told you, would it even matter? Would it answer questions, give you closure?

Do you even care?

OK.

> *She leans forward, once again searching for words.*

I know what you're thinking.

And in the deepest, hidden, most cynical part of your brain, you know what I mean when I say that.

> *She puts two fingers to her left temple.*

(Almost whispering.) Please don't freak out!

> *She closes her eyes.*

'I shouldn't be here. I shouldn't be doing this. This is a bad idea. What am I doing here? What is she doing here? What, she just wants to talk? Let me guess, this is one of those closure things she read about in a magazine. I mean...'

She opens her eyes, staring straight at him.

'Of course I care you know. I dunno. Since when does she have short hair? She looks great in that dress. Wait, what am I...? Maybe I should leave. Should I say something? Did she really think that all it would take was coffee and a tiny slice of...wait a second, did she just...what the hell how is she doing...'

She jumps out of her seat and steps back, putting her hand out in front of her – to keep him back? To stop him leaving?

I always wanted to tell you.
I just, I couldn't figure out how. Or when. It's all starting to make sense now. Isn't it?

Sheila

Iman Qureshi

> **A hard-working student finds out that her study partner received a higher grade, whilst she did all the work. For ages 18 and above.**

So we think it's a boyfriend...

Miles, this isn't the time for kissing.
Oh don't give me that hurt look.
Seriously, that boy.
Right, here we go. To do:

- Cancel dinner.
- Vac scheme applications.
- References for history dissertation.
- Organise speaker for next union talk. Female. BAME. Obvs.
- Text that lazy idiot 'Antonio' from Ancient Civilizations tutorial back about our presentation at the history society.
- Rehearse for ukulele campus flashmob.
- Prep for Germany's position in Model United Nations special session on Rwandan genocide.
- Write letter to MP expressing concern regarding housing benefit cuts for 18-21s.
- Ring council to ask why mum's benefits have been delayed.
- Ring mum, I suppose.

- Check exam results at nine – alarm set.

Miles – are you humping me?! What did I just say?
No, no licking either. No licking, no licking –
Ohhh, OK then – good boy, who's a good boy who's a
good boy. Brrrrrrrrr.

Throws a ball.

Get the ball, get the ball!

Beat.

Miles is a dog obviously. I don't have time for a relationship.
Which reminds me:

- Delete Tinder. Seriously just delete it.

Looks at the limbs MILES has just licked.

- Ugh and I'll have to shower now I guess.

Life is mental busy, but this little guy is the one thing
keeping me sane. Even if he's such hard work. Black girls
don't have corgis people tell me. The Queen has corgis.
Oh are you looking after him? Who's this dog's owner?
Like I'm some maid that walks dogs for rich people. But
they're wrong. I'm a black girl who has a corgi – who
says I can't? No one can tell me what I can and can't
have, what I can and can't do.

Pshhh, I hate that attitude you know? Can't do this can't
do that, it's cos I'm black, the world is against me. Work.
Work hard. Still not getting anywhere? Then work even
harder cos it's obviously still not enough. Want to get
places? Cut out all the crap. Nights out with friends.

Boyfriend. Tinder – delete that stuff. Dinners. Food even if you have to. Cut it all out. That's what I've done and look at me.

Text sound.

You've got to be joking. Antonio, Antonio from Ancient Civilisations, is 'sick'. Hungover more like. Classic example of not working hard enough. Antonio gives it the bare minimum. This whole term that boy has been copying my notes, borrowing my books, asking to meet up for study groups so that I can tell him all the stuff he's missed. I swear, that boy is only on the history society for the CV cred. I know exams are over and all, but this is a joke. MILES STOP. Sorry, baby, sorry, sorry.

OK, it's fine. I got this. I wrote it all anyway. I've got this. ARGH. No chill, it's fine. It's fine. Right. Exam results. Then practice this presentation I now need to do all by myself, without any help from Antonio. Man up Sheila. Man up. No, excuse me sorry – Woman up. Yeah that's right. You get those wibbly wobbly weak arse ovaries together and woman up.

No, I'll need more time. Right, ukuele practice – sorry babes, you gotta go. Got to prioritise, cut out all the crap remember? Work harder. No sunny afternoon for me.

(Texting.) Hey girls, sorry not gonna make it today. Something's come up. Have a good time, I'll catch up on practice I promise. Kiss kiss. Send.

Does that sound too vague? Like an excuse. They're gonna hate me. This isn't the first time. I sound just like flakey Antonio. No Sheila, if he can do it so can you. At least you have an actual proper excuse. Rah, but I just feel so bad.

Alarm goes.

Oh no. OK. This is it, this is it. Final year. Final exams. Final results. Excepting dissertation of course, but I know I've smashed that.

Logs onto the results portal on her phone. Long pause.

There's got to be a mistake. This is... No. I mean – I worked my arse off. I literally, I mean, I literally broke out with a rash on my bum because I was working so hard, sitting in that steaming library all year. This isn't my student number – this has got to be... *(Pause.)* No.

Phone rings.

Antonio? Hey – what did I get? Oh I – uh – haven't checked yet. *(Beat.)* You got a first? Oh – congrats. That's – great. *(Beat.)* Oh yeah – you're welcome. Yeah I'll uh – let you know when I find out. Celebrate? tonight? Umm – no, no I can't. Everyone's going? I really can't. *(Beat.)* Wait, weren't you sick?

Sign

Ross Willis

> **A school boy learns to read with the help of his dinner lady. For school ages.**

'What's that?' I say.
'Read the sign' she says.
'Or you could tell me' I say.
'Spaghetti bolognese' she says.
'I ain't EVER seen spaghetti bolognese look like that' I say.

'MOVE ALONG JOEL!'

And that is how me and Miss Smith the dinner lady greet each other every single school day.

She didn't want to be a dinner lady, obviously. She wanted to be a pianist like Beethoven and shit. She plays piano at my church and we may pretend we don't know each other. Hands movin' fasta than I've ever seen 'em serve food.

'What's that?' I say.
'Read the sign' she says.
'Or you could tell me' I say.
'Shepherd's pie' she says.
'I ain't EVER seen shepherd's pie which looks like that!'

'MOVE ALONG JOEL!'

Sunday. I'm in church and Miss Smith is playin' piano again. We're singing my favourite gospel, I don't read the lyrics but I love the way it sounds.

'What's that?' I say.
'Read the sign' she says.
'Or you could tell me' I say.
'I see you mumblin' lyrics in church. The others might not hear but I do!' she says.
And her face drops and she whispers *'Can you not read?'*
I say nothin'. I am nothin'.

Sunday. I'm at the church social and we've got Hobnobs and I am pumped because they are my favourite biscuits yo! Pastor Mike comes up to me, shakes my hand, and we chat about school and the weather and then he asks, *'Joel, maybe you'd like to do a reading at a service next month?'* I see Miss Smith starin', mouth wide open, bits of Hobnobs splutterin' out. *'Would you like that Joel? Joel would you like to read next month?'* I say nothin'. I am nothin'.

'What's that?' I say.
'Read the sign' she says.
'Or you could tell me' I say.
'Read the sign' she says.
'Or you could tell me' I say.
'Read the sign' she says. *'Read the sign'* she says. *'Read the sign'* she says. And inside I am beggin' her to stop! I say nothin'. I am nothin'.

I skip lunch for the rest of the week. Food tastes like shit anyway.

Sunday. Church. I love that it goes beyond words and it's about what you feel in your heart.

They are all at the social and I'm out back smokin' cuz I don't wanna see her. Suddenly I hear a squark. *'Give us one Joel'*, it's only Miss Smith ain't it!

I say nah so she grabs it out my hands and starts puffin' and puffin' and puffin'. *'How have you managed to hide it?'* she says. An' I tell her everythin', I tell her everyone just presumes I can read, so I let them presume, tell her I don't care.

As I tell her everythin', I realise it's the first time I've actually seen her hair up close as she's mostly got that stupid hat on. It's grey but it's like she's brushed it for hours, like she's made an effort. Like this is the only time the world gets to see her hair. *'Wouldn't you like to read at a service Joel?'*, *'Nah people would just make fun.'* I say.

She puts out the cigarette. *'Joel this isn't a place where people come to insult or hate, they come here to love. I'll help you every week after school.'* She says it like it's a statement, not a question.

An' we start. An' we go on. An' we stop. An' we start. An' we go on. Day after day. Week after week. And when I got angry she made me laugh. And when I got sad she made me smile. And what I used to see as symbols and squiggles I'm now seein' as sounds. And what I used to see as a frumpy woman I'm now seein' as a friend.

It's the day of the readin'. Sweaty sweaty palms. Pastor Mike says, *'And now Joel is going to read something for us'*

They all politely clap, Miss Smith lets out a whistle and then instantly regrets it.

And I start. And I hear Miss Smith's voice in my head. *'Joel this isn't a place where people come to hate, they come here to love. They. Come. Here To. Love.'*

And the symbols and squiggles become sounds and the sounds vibrate all around that church. They come out slow and confused but they come out.

And the listeners. They came to love. And when I get lost, they love and when I get confused they love. Don't get a chance to chat to Miss Smith cuz everyone wants to congratulate me.

I sees her at school the next week. Hand attackin the lumpiest mash potato I've ever seen. She looks up.

'What's that?' I say. *'Read the sign'* she says *'Roast chicken'* I read. *'But it looks like shit.'*

And she smiles.

Spare a Minute?

Ayesha Manazir Siddiqi

> **A street charity fundraiser is all about helping people. Sometimes it's putting money in a bucket. Sometimes it's selling pills. Age stated in monologue as 20 years old.**

KORRA, 20, a street charity fundraiser, is on the street with her bucket, soliciting passers-by.

Excuse me, sir, do you have a minute to spare for the blind? That's fine. Have a nice day. Ma'am, hello. Did you know that one in ten people in the youuuu...kay, OK.

This happens. Especially on the cold days. They walk right through you. It's easy to take it personal, especially on your first day. But don't. Just remember, it's not you, it's them. Hi, Sssss – irrr...

Don't tell Darren but I like to fuck with them sometimes. Ma'am, we're collecting donations for haircuts gone wrong. Have you been a victim yourself? They don't care about starving orphans, these fuckers. The closer you get to their own shitty lives, the more likely they are to stop. Hello sir, a donation for low battery lives on iphones? BAM. He stops. Just kidding, Sir. It's for the blind. OK then. Nine times out of ten, they roll their eyes and walk on. Hypocrites.

How long are you thinking of doing this kind of work, then? Me, I won't be here long. I'm gonna take it out of their taxes soon. See, I'm studying political science at the moment. And I'm student union rep, I do this work... the plan is to get to a place where I decide where the money goes. I mean, how many times have you seen someone who looks like me, talks like me, up there? That's what we need more of, don't you think so? First thing, I'll make uni fees cheaper. Then spend on anti-racism. And give to the NHS. That's important. Mental health services, that's important. Mum, you know, she struggles. 'Manic psychotic depression' the doctors call it. It means she'd be off at all hours, that I'd come home sometimes to find her dancing around the kitchen table. But there's no music playing. And worse things too. Worse. But she's OK now. On her meds. Forgets to take them sometimes, but overall she's doing really well. Yeah. And those Eton white boys in power, what do they know where the money needs to go? What do they know of our struggles, right?

Madam a minute for...you didn't pick the best day to start, did you? It'll pick up though. Don't worry...so yeah, what was I saying? Make uni cheaper. My fees are nine thousand pounds a year. Nine thousand. Where are normal people supposed to get that money from? So I take the ones she doesn't take. The pills, I mean. The anti-depression meds. I pocket them. And I sell them. She's forgotten to take them, and other people need them. And I need to study. And it's all for a good cause so...yeah. Sue me. How else are people like me meant to... And I know. I know you saw me pocket that fiver. I saw you see me do it. But if I take a pound or two out of this sometimes (*donation bucket*), what's wrong with that? It's all adding up for me to get to the top, to fight in your corner, you know?

Sometimes, we pop them. The pills. Days like this feel like fucking rainbows when you're on them. I'd never sell them to colleagues, of course not. But sometimes, when they play their cards right, you know...anyway. Less talk, more work. Here now, have a go on the next one yourself. Hi. Sir? Can my friend here help you change the world?

Standing Ovation

Titilola Dawudu

> **A woman supports her husband's acting dreams. And she's not in the least bit jealous. For ages 25 and above.**

Damn, we're late. It looks like it's already started. We're gonna have to sit somewhere at the back – oh, look no. There's plenty of seats. What there's one, two, three, four...nine people here. Great. Nine people – nope eleven including us. Thanks for coming with me. I couldn't bear to see another one alone then have to come up with something good to say about it. I've got this down so far – 'wow babe, you were really good. Especially in the scene where...' Then I fill in the blanks. It could be the scene where he is just about to commit suicide, but is stopped just in time – or is he? Dun, dun, dun. Or the scene where he has a breakdown. And wants to end his life, but is stopped just in time. Dun, dun, dun. They're all the same these student plays he performs in. And he keeps on friggin' doing them. 'I believe in the project. It resonates with me.' How does it resonate with him? He's got a good life, doesn't pay any bills. I have a great job in IT and have already been promoted twice, having only been there for three years. And I'm the youngest in my department.

I'm not being bitter! Why'd you say that? I love what I do and I'm glad to support him. I am!

Look – that was then. Yeah, we met at drama school, but ultimately we had different dreams. Plus I grew up. We married young and someone needed to be responsible.

Shall we go in now? Oh wait – I can hear him do his monologue bit. He rehearsed this with me a thousand times. I love that he's passionate about acting. You know, 'cause sometimes with my job – it's stressful and I wouldn't say I'm passionate about it – but I'm good at it and I've made strides – I'm the youngest in my – sorry, I said that already, didn't I?

Honestly – I love that he gets to do this... We both do what we love and that's good. I know I can moan about it and seeing all these plays, but he's happy and I'm happy. I love my job – I'm good at it.

What do you mean, 'Why are you trying to convince yourself?' Convince myself of what? No – no – you've got it wrong. If I had the chance would I act? Would I want to be where he is right now? No, of course not. This is his dream, not mine. And I couldn't act now anyway. I'm too rusty. I'd have to take an acting course and how will I do that with my job? I mean, I know there's some classes at the local college on a Tuesday night, but what would I do that for? No – it's fine. It's fine. This is his thing not mine.

Why don't you believe me? I am being honest with you. And I couldn't really do anything about it, even if I wanted to. Why? Because of my job...and the life we live. We've got bills and...

OK, OK. You're right. You're right. But please don't tell him? Look – it doesn't matter. It's OK. I'm happy with how things are. He's happy. It's OK. Really. Now's not the time – oh crap – it's the interval. Here he comes. Don't say anything. Promise?

'Wow babe, you were really good. Especially in the scene where…'

Stay Vigilant

Guleraana Mir

> A homeless man is being interviewed about a killer murdering criminals – a killer people suspect is a homeless man. For ages 18 and above.

JACK nervously hopping from one foot to another. He tries to make himself look presentable, tucking and untucking his shirt.

Sorry, just...nervous, never been on telly before. Wanna make a good impression. *(Beat.)*

Are my eyes bloodshot? I'm not sleeping very well, got to stay vigilant. Especially right now... Never know who's coming after you, who you've pissed off. Sorry, can I say pissed off? Oh, sorry. I won't when we're – Oh what, now? OK. Um.

> *He nods in time and mouths three, two, one, freezing in an awkward grin, half-waving to the camera.*

Hi. *(Beat.)* Yeah, it's been about three years now, I think. *(Beat.)* It was a series of bad choices I made at home, at school and I – oh, my advice? Don't apologise. Cos you know, it's not your fault you end up homeless... It's not though, not really, but it becomes second nature, apologising. Saying sorry for taking up space, for begging, for...

Course there's crime, and yeah it's tempting, yeah. Course. You see people with nice stuff and... I'm not part of some organised crime gang! Just cos I've got a mobile phone you think...? Yeah my phone's nicer than some people's but I didn't steal it. You don't want to give me anything lady, you don't have to, but don't be accusing me of – the best? I'm invisible. Everyone chooses to, tries really hard to, not see me. Has its perks. It's surprising what you can get away with when people don't notice you.

They think that killer's homeless, don't they?

That's why you're here, pretending to interview us, pretending to care. Just digging for clues, aren't you? Well, I think he's doing the city a favour. He only kills criminals. Other murderers, rapists, drug dealers the ones that slip through the legal system. If the police did a better job at catching the bad guys then he wouldn't have to... I mean it's not like he likes killing, I imagine. I can't imagine he likes killing.

It's not like you get a rush out of it, do you? *(Laughs.)* I can't comment on how the killer may or may not feel, I can only... I just know that if I spent ages helping the police build a case against the person responsible for my, for this...but he still got away with it, that might be enough, might...to tip me over the edge. You know, just... just saying that I get it. Not all superheroes wear capes. Someone's got to look out for us. Someone's got to stay vigilant.

Stuffed

Tessa Hart

> A mental health patient finds solace in a stuffed mouse and other stuffed toys. For ages 16 and above.

(Talking to a cuddly toy mouse whilst putting some of the stuffing back into it.) And what shall we call you? Eleanor? Jennifer? Destiny?

I like meaningful names. Like mine, Hope.

And you shall be Destiny and this is your destiny. Stuffed in here with me.

Destiny and Hope. Both stuck in here, stuffed. You literally, and me figuratively. I know the difference between those two words. Lots of people don't, but I'm pretty clever for my age.

You're lucky, you know Destiny. I did consider eating you instead of stuffing you, but I don't think mice taste very nice. Besides mum will be here soon to bring me real food, which will probably taste better than you...

You'll get to sit on the shelf over there, next to your other stuffed little friends...you're so lucky to have friends, you know!

Wouldn't it be fun if you were alive, like a real mouse! Then you could be *my* friend and I could keep you as a kind of pet. Would be more exciting too, I do get really bored in here.

Maybe the next one of your little friends that I catch will be a real living mouse! I'll put him in a cage and I'll call him Trash! And I'll treat him like trash, because that's what you get treated like when you live in a cage that you can't get out of.

I used to have a real pet, you know? A tortoise called Henry. Forgot to feed him, he starved to death. Well, I didn't really forget, but I had nothing to feed him with, so it was the same thing. He got really stinky when he was dead so mum threw him away.

I hope mum comes soon I'm quite hungry. If she forgot to feed me I would starve to death. And then I would get stinky but there's no one here to throw me away... only you, Destiny.

Maybe I should really have eaten you, Destiny? Or maybe I'll eat your boyfriend Trash when he comes.

Did you have any babies Destiny? Are they slowly starving to death now because Mummy isn't coming back? Mummies shouldn't do that to their kids, they always have to take care of them. Always. Even when they're sick and even when it makes them sad.

My mum always still comes to feed and take care of me and sometimes the social worker comes and sometimes the nurse. It's like... I'm their pet... But maybe they've run out of food too, like I did for Henry, because no one's come in a long while now.

But you know what Destiny? It doesn't matter anymore because really soon I'm going to get out of here and join the tiny people out there. I watch them every day looking down through the window. People and children and dogs and cars and sometimes bikes too; and some people walk and some people run and some people are mummies with babies in their buggies and they're always walking really fast...and they don't even know I'm here, watching them... And when I look up through the window when the sky is clear, I can see that funny building in the distance; I think they call it a gherkin. And I can see the sunset every night, but I can't see the sunrise. I can see the sun die every night but I never see it being born, yet it always seems to come back somehow. And sometimes, at night I can see the moon; I think it's getting bigger lately.

And one day, when I'm ready, I'm going to go out and join the people out there. And I'm going to rush around with them, like I have important things to do, and I'll see the sunrise and maybe I'll even climb on top of the gherkin.

'Til then I'm going to wait for mum to bring me some food. I'm really quite hungry. Let's wait for her Destiny, she'll be here soon... I hope.

Take The Money

Bushra Laskar

> **A man in need of a bone marrow transplant is willing to pay any amount. Age stated in monologue as 45 years old.**

ZAIN RIAD, forty-five, dressed in a smart suit. In a crowded café.

No. Absolutely not. We agreed all of this weeks ago. I'd rather just pay you and do it that way. I'll give you half now and the rest after the op.

Listen Amit, I know you mean well but you have absolutely no right to even suggest that. You know how rare it is to find a donor for people like me, like us. There's no reason to think my birth parents will even be a match anyway so I'll just be wasting time. My time. Seven months, Amit. That's all I've got left unless we do the transplant. I don't understand why you're doing this. Do you want more money? Is that what this is? Ok, fine. Name your price.

And what if I do find my biological parents? Why the hell should they care what happens to me now? They don't know me from Adam. They turned their backs on me once and yes OK they may have had their reasons but you really think they're just going to hand over their bone marrow on a platter? Just like that?

These past few months have been hell, you know that right? And you want me to...

This is none of your concern, Amit. I should never have told you about them. This is just a business transaction between us. You donate your bone marrow and I make you a bank transfer. Two, actually. No one will ever know, and we both get what we want. Are you now going back on your word to hold me to ransom like this?

Amit, listen, I know you think you're helping me but you're not, so just sign the contract and take the money, OK?

Please.

Taliya
Mediah Ahmed

> **A woman with bipolar disorder channels Nina Simone to get over a traumatic event. Age stated in monologue as 21 years old.**

TALIYA, 21, student in Law, bipolar.

TALIYA sings the introduction and refrain from Nina Simone's 'Feeling Good' as if performing in front of thousands.

'What the hell was that?' he goes.

(TALIYA as Nina.) I do what the hell I want. When I am on that stage. I am free. I can be whoever the fuck I want. No one can stop me. Not even you, Andrew.

That's what I really want to say.

Music has been a burden and a joy for as long as I can remember. That's what I really want to say.

Each song I sing is an emotional message, which means using everything I've got inside, sometimes to barely make a note, or if I have to strain to sing, I sing. That's what I really want to say.

So sometimes I sound like gravel, and sometimes I sound like coffee and cream. That's what I really want to say to Andrew.

I say nothing.

He says: 'You are where you are because of me. I built you up, I can also bring you down.'

That's true.

'Go see Dr Morgan.'

'Do you know where you are?' Dr Morgan asks.
I just performed in front of millions of people.
I just got raped by Andrew.
Dr Morgan wants to know: Who is Andrew?
My husband.
'I see. What is your name?' the Doctor asks.
Nina. Nina Simone.

'Taliya,' the doctor says. 'Your name is Taliya. My name is Dr Morgan. What is the last thing you can remember?'

I remember......the rave...... I repelled everyone like iron filings around magnets. It was my fault. I didn't take my medication and all hell broke loose.
Nina you came to me, you sang to me and no one believed me.
Andrew?
You were supposed to protect me. But I didn't think I would need protecting from you.

> *TALIYA sings lines from Nina Simone's 'Sinnerman'.*

> *Pause.*

You understand me, don't you Nina?

The Birds

Lynsey Martenstyn

> **A man who trains homing pigeons uses one to find a woman he likes. Age stated in monologue as mid 40s.**

RAJ, mid 40s, mid 2000s, hipster attire: keffiyeh, ironic t-shirt and brightly coloured large rucksack. On a doorstep. Knocks on the door.

Stacey! Long time. You look – right. OK. Look.
I know what it looks like. Basically, I can explain.

Nervous laugh.

Funny story actually. The thing is –

Nervous laugh.

I know it doesn't seem funny at the moment. Basically – I'm a nice guy – colleagues at work tell me so. Like Beatrice and Octavia. They're all, y'know: 'Thanks for fetching my Pret, Raj', 'Super-duper tea, Raj'.

I'm a good person. I am a good – look, everyone has a vice, right? Bet you have. I don't drink, smoke, gamble. I recycle, properly. I vote, drink organic, putrid green smoothies every morning. I'm a decent person. But. The pigeons? I can explain.

The idea first came to me, a Christmas eight years ago.

My mum goes big at Christmas. Ten foot, robotic neon Santa in the front garden. Lights wrap the house like a rave-bound boa constrictor. Endless Twiglets. Almost a middle finger to the twitchy-curtain twats in the village, who assume we don't 'do' Christmas. *(Beat.)* So, everyone's asleep. I'm up, of course, celebrating the birth of Jesus by watching a War World One documentary about spies. That's when I see them. War pigeons. These regular grey pigeons with tiny cameras strapped to their little, noble chests. Incredible.

So, I'm driving back that year and take a spontaneous detour through Watford. Mad, I know. On a whim, I'd called this bloke from Gumtree who was selling a few pigeons.

That January was especially long, dark and depressing. I'd finished *Breaking Bad*. Thought it was 'meh'. I missed my family. To cheer myself up, I began training the pigeons. Basically, a homing pigeon will know how to get from A to B, but not back. It's a one-way thing. However, I judiciously trained each pigeon to fly from A to B and back, just like the Signal Pigeon Corps in the U.S. Army. I've got a book on them. I can email you a PDF, if you – ? So. Yeah. I trained each pigeon to go to a different, specific destination.

It took months, but I'm no quitter. Basically, you girls all lie about your age. D'you know how hard it is to find a woman's address, without a valid date of birth? Let's just say, you could call me James Bond 2.0. *(Realisation. Quicker.)* Yeah. So then, I attached teeny cameras to the pigeons and linked them to my phone. And that was seven years ago. *(Pause. Beat.)*

And that's where you come in, Stacey!

Remember when we first met, when I was dating Isobelle? Your sister, yeah. I always thought you were, well, more aesthetically pleasing.

So, I bought another pigeon. Mabel.

And found your address.

The Everlasting Tan

Abraham Adeyemi

> **A hairdresser has to explain her identity after being constantly questioned about it. Age stated in monologue as 17 years old.**

MEL, *seventeen, black.*

A hair salon.

(*To customer.*) Course I can do it babes, I'm a professional hairdresser. Not white hair, black hair, green hair, just hair, like any hair. Professionally. I've got you. We're gonna have you looking absolutely fab by the time I'm done with you, whether it's Katie, Becky, Vicky or me, Melanie – but you can call me Mel – Holly's Hair-idise always gets it right. My clients never complain.

> *Silence.*

(*To audience.*) Do you identify as Asian... Black... White... or Other?

> *Pause.*

As in, do I. How do I identify.

> *MEL stares sternly out into the distance, almost looking spaced out.*

Well, like, it isn't as black and white (*sniggers*) – *as black and white* as that, init.

Pause.

But as you're asking me what do I identify as...

Silence.

White.

Pause.

It's not what it looks like.

Silence.

(To customer.) Not being funny babes but you sound a bit posh. You're not from round 'ere, are you?

Pause.

Ohhhhhh, you're from THOOOSE sides. Nice round there. All them fancy restaurants that nobody can afford. Well, I guess you can afford them. We been getting more people like you here, you know, ever since Holly had that interview in Time Out. Going big time, now, Holly's Hair-idise. We're almost fully booked into next year!

Pause.

Now let me see. Hmm...

Pause.

Hmm... D'you want me to be honest with you? I'm really not... Hang on a sec...

MEL pulls out her mobile phone and swipes through pictures.

Found it! This, this, this, this is the one! Have a look? Perfect for you, ain't it babes. If we just *(holds customer's hair)* have it a little shorter here, and blonde like you wanted it. You are going to kill them. SLAY.

Pause.

No, as in, literally, when I'm done with you, you're gonna walk out of those doors, onto the high street and pedestrians are gonna fall to the ground. Cars are gonna crash, people gonna die and go to hell for lusting over you, oh you are gonna look absolutely INCREDIBLE!

Silence.

(To audience.) Sorry, where were we... Coleen and Peter Crater, mother and father to one, Mel Crater, myself. Yeah, wicked for the puberty jokes when my face had more fucking holes than a sieve.

Pause.

When I was younger, like too young to remember younger, we went on holiday to Dubai – *(To customer.)* Oh you've been to Dubai as well, babes? I wanna go again, now I'm older you know. So I can remember it. I hear they chop off your tits if you show a bit of skin, cheeky bikini and they're getting their knickers in a twist about it?! Not sure about that part...

Pause.

(To audience.) It was 2002, so I was like two, and it was the hottest its eeeever been there. As in, ever ever. Fifty-two degrees! Like, I struggle if it even goes past twenty-

three degrees, end up looking like I just came out of a pool and that, don't I.

Pause.

Anyway, don't ask me why 'cause I don't know and Dubai wasn't even popping like that back then but we were there for about two weeks and that's how it came about.

Pause.

That's how I got my everlasting tan.

Silence.

(To customer.) He didn't!

Pause.

Nooooo! You've gotta dump him, sis. Look at you! You deserve better. Dump. *(Claps.)* Him. *(Claps.)*

Pause.

Almost there now, almost there.

Pause.

Told you I'd have you looking fab, almost there! Why are you so surprised?

Silence.

Oh honey, no, this is just a tan. *(To audience.)* God, I really hope she doesn't make this awkward. *(To customer.)* You know, like when you go on holiday, somewhere hot, skin gets darker *(points at face)*. Except it never went. *(To audience.)* Right, she's definitely making it awkward.

Pause.

Yeah, I get it. Most people look like that when I say it, but after a while they get their heads around it. I mean it's easy for me, a bit. Like unless I say something, nobody knows but imagine, their whole lives, from when I was that young, people asking mum and dad why they have a black baby and all that.

Pause.

Change subject.

Pause.

Except she just can't let it go...

MEL sighs heavily.

(To customer.) Yeah, I'm being serious.

MEL balks.

... Hang on... Did you... Did you actually just –

Silence.

MEL slowly inhales and exhales.

Silence.

MEL is out front of the hairdressers. She lights up a cigarette and begins to smoke.

(To audience.) Who does that bitch think she's talking to like that? Who the hell is she to question my identity? That's why you can't get too fucking friendly with these

customers. 'It's the Holly's Hair-idise way.' Well yeah, but when you give a bitch an inch and too many smiles she runs fucking miles... Telling me I'm a confused little girl and I don't know who I am... Is she mad?

Silence.

Do you identify as Asian... Black... White... or Other?

Pause.

It's not as easy as that.

MEL combs through her hair with her fingers.

(To Holly.) Look Holly, just give me a minute, alright?

MEL walks away.

(To audience.) Says so much, don't it, me working here. Can make you whoever you want to be. That's why I've always loved it. That's how I ended up here.

Pause.

Sorry. But I'm not sorry. It wasn't her place. She doesn't know me. She doesn't know my story. Who is she to tell me who I am – FUCK!

MEL runs back into the store, halts and stares in horror.

Shit shit shit shit!

Pause.

(To Holly.) Holly, let me help – please, let – fuck fuck fuck, I'm so dumb...

Silence.

(To audience.) Why did you let it get to you Mel? Why didn't you just keep your cool?! You're not new to this...

Silence.

I've screwed up. I've screwed up sooooo bad. Her skin, it's flipping purple, by the edges –

Silence.

(To customer.) I'm so sorry, no, please, calm down – OK no I know you can't keep calm but it's gonna be alri...
(To audience.) You didn't need to react. How was she to know, how is anyone to know, when all they can know is what they see? Yet you wanna be a bloody idiot and overreact like they're the ones not being logical...

Silence.

(To Holly.) Holly, I'm... I'm sorry... This wouldn't normally... And I'm good, like really good... But the customers love me, you love me, I love... Please, I need...

(To audience.) Do you identify as Asian... Black... White... or Other?

Pause.

Are my mum and my dad, my mum and my dad and I, like them, are white... Or do I accept that I've been lied to my whole life, that they're not my parents, and that I have no fucking clue who I am?

Silence.

I'm packing my shit – Do you identify as Asian... Black...
White... or Other? I'm home – Do you identify as Asian...
Black... White... or Other? But I don't go in. I sit on the
wall. And I cry. Do you identify as Asian... Black... White...
or Other? And cry. And cry. And cry. Do you identify as
Asian... Black... White... or Other? But you can't cry for
too long. Do you identify as Asian... Black... White... or
Other? Because tears don't pay the bills. Do you identify
as Asian... Black... White... or Other? Guess I better
get started on the job applications. Do you identify as
Asian... Black... White... or Other? And start filling out
these long, boring forms that ask for everything that's
already on your CV... Not forgetting the equality forms...
Do you identify as Asian... Black... White... or Other?

The Fan

Mina Barber

> **A police officer deals with a grieving father who has lost his daughter. For ages 25 and above.**

An office in a police station.

SHAZIA enters and sits down. She addresses the audience as if she's speaking to her superior.

Morning Ma'am, you asked to speak to me? The incident? On the estate? Er...yes Ma'am, it was a noise disturbance call out. The gentleman had been playing music on a loop at a high volume, the neighbours called some concern about a child at the property, they thought they heard some screaming but couldn't tell over the music. The music? Oh it's one of my favourites, Taylor Swift, my girls say I'm too old for it! Sorry Ma'am, yes of course, the incident. So, we pulled up at the property and the music was at a very high volume enough to be a nuisance.

> *SHAZIA stands up and pretends she's knocking at a front door; she's transported back to the incident earlier. Music plays in the background as if it's muffled.*

HELLO! HELLO! MR ADAMS! MY NAME'S OFFICER SHAZIA CHOUDHURY! CAN YOU PLEASE PLEASE TURN THE MUSIC DOWN SO WE CAN TALK? MR ADAMS!

She breathes a sigh of relief as the music is turned down, she waits but the man doesn't come to the door.

Mr Adams, Sir, I know that you're there. I just wanted to have a chat, if you could just...

She kneels down to look through the letterbox.

Sir I can see you, if you could just turn down the television too and just come to the door.

Er...we have reason to believe that there is a child at the property; we need to ensure her safety.

SHAZIA suddenly jumps back; she collects herself and sits back up.

That's very charming of you Sir, 'Paki Islam Bitch', I'll have to remember that one, that even beats the names my ex-husband used to call me, and I can promise you, he had a few. If you could just let me in we can talk.

She carefully opens the letterbox again.

... Oh hello sweetheart, you OK? Yeah? Is that your Daddy in there? Yeah? Good girl.

SHAZIA suddenly jumps back again as if the man has approached and kicked the door.

No, no, Sir, no need to kick the door. I was just checking she was OK I'm sure you wouldn't do anything to hurt her. What was that?

SHAZIA opens the letterbox again.

Yes I have seen the news Sir, I know you probably feel

like your daughter isn't safe, I can tell you I hugged my daughters very tight that night too, oh, you have two daughters too? Yeah my two are a funny pair, one's always got her head stuck in a book, she'll be alright, then there's the other one, selfies and contouring, no, I know I'm lucky. It's hard to keep them safe. So you said you have two, is your other daughter there? I'm so sorry, are you OK Sir? Sweetheart let me in and your daddy and me can talk, I can see he's very upset. That's it good girl.

SHAZIA stands and tidies herself, she then goes to speak as a door opens. She sits back down on the chair as if she's back in the room with her superior.

He had been watching loops of news reports of the bomb at the arena, he lost his other daughter in a car accident last year, someone just drove into them. She was a big Taylor Swift fan. He was just frightened. I entered the property, no, no, he didn't come at me Ma'am the gentleman just well, fell to the floor and curled up in a ball. I don't know Ma'am, I put my arms around him, and then, I, I just started, not full pelt or nothin' just gentle and he just cried, and cried.

She kneels back down as if she's back in the flat with the man. She has her arms around him.

She starts to sing a low voice version of Taylor Swift's 'Shake it off' as if she's comforting a child.

The First Wednesday of the Eighth Month

Olivia Furber

> A junior doctor, about to start her first day at work, has recently been diagnosed with bipolar disorder and doesn't want anyone to know. For ages 25 and above.

She is having breakfast with her housemate, they are both junior doctors. They are both about to begin their first round at their first hospital after qualifying. Over the weekend she was diagnosed with bipolar disorder and she plans on concealing it.

Don't you think it's a bit fucked up that we all start work on the same day? All of us new doctors on the same day? I bet mortality rates rise in the first week of August. Seriously, tell your mum to come and get checked next week instead.

> *Her housemate stands up to get something from the fridge.*

Can you grab the milk whilst you're up? Almond. Not cow.

I decided not to tell them. It's too risky. They won't find out because I know a woman who's a senior consultant and she did me a favour by taking all the tests then submitting them to another doctor under a different name.

Her housemate returns to the table and puts down the almond milk.

You know almond milk is one pound cheaper in Aldi?

Look, I'm keeping a mood diary so I can track the condition: 'Today I feel a bit nervous – naturally it's my first day – a bit tired – but nothing caffeine can't solve – and generally optimistic. Smiley face'.

I'm my own first patient. I'll know when it's necessary to medicate. I actually slightly regret not choosing psychiatry now, I've always had a worry my fingers were a bit too fat for surgery anyway.

Trust me, they would judge me if I told them. Remember when I was really down during final term and I spoke to Dr Marsh? I was trying to be responsible for myself and for any patients I came into contact with. I said, 'I'm too tired to learn. All I'm achieving is just existing for long periods of time.' And what did he say? 'Of course you're stressed. It's your final term. You're a girl.' This man has no emotional thermostat. In his eyes you can't be a person and a doctor.

Don't look at me like that. Like in a pitying way. It's fine. I feel fine, really. And now I've got a diagnosis I know how to handle it.

Oh come on. Stop looking at me like that! That is not me, I am not like that woman. I'm not going to set myself on fire and kill myself. That's not going to happen. But how you're looking at me right now confirms why there is no point in telling anyone about this.

She clears her food from the table in preparation to leave.

We're going to be late.

The Honest Truth

Naomi Joseph

> **A Jewish man is asking his girlfriend to accept his beliefs. Age stated in monologue as 28 years old.**

JONATHAN, twenty-eight, Jewish.

A park. JONATHAN is with his girlfriend Sarah.

Look... When I think about the future I imagine getting married in a synagogue. I see mezuzahs on the doors of our home. I see my grandma telling us off when we get the order of the Seder wrong on Passover!

Being Jewish...it – it's more than a religion, it's a culture too. It's the food, the community, the people. It's what I've known, it's what I've grown up with.

Sarah, I want to create a Jewish home. And I don't want to do that by myself.

I also don't want to change a good thing for the sake of a technicality. Once upon a time finding a Jewish girl was the goal. It's nice to share that common ground with someone from the start, y'know?

Plus in Judaism lineage goes through the mother. I didn't want to lose out. But now, more importantly, I don't want to lose you.

And I'm not saying it's easy but it can work! Like...there's this guy at my shul. He schleps his kids to Cheder on a Sunday. He does security for the synagogue – and you know what? The man is an atheist! Yet he does it to support his wife, to be there for his kids.

Look I will never ask you to convert. That's your personal decision. I'll never force any of this on you.

So no...you not being Jewish isn't a deal-breaker for me. My parents aren't gonna shut you out and my Rabbi won't turn you away at the door. And I promise I will never ask you to compromise your own beliefs. I'm just asking...is there space for mine?

The N Word

Titilola Dawudu

> **At an open mic night, a friend sabotages another to get the spotlight. For ages 18 and above.**

Thanks for saving me a seat. Keisha's nervous.

You know she asked me to write for her 'cause I like writing and I do some poetry and stuff. Even though she wants to be a rapper I don't think writing's her strong point. And she says lots of rappers have other people write for them. So I said, 'yeah I'll do it.'

I'm er, not sure when she's on.

Starts clapping.

You've gotta clap for everyone. It's what you do here.

I've been to these open mics nights before but this one's the best. People get signed performing here. Keisha says that this is her big chance.

So she wanted us here for support. She says we've got to clap the loudest. She's scared people will boo her, but there's no booing – that's not allowed at this club. Everyone claps or clicks their fingers, even if it's crap. And there's no N word allowed. That's their policy.

I'm sure she's on soon. Just chill out, yeah?

Keisha's pissed about the no N word. I was just backstage with her. She says that you should be allowed to say what you want. It's 'expressing ourselves'.

And I'm like, 'yeah.' And she's like, 'when you say it without the 'er' part – it's not a slave thing anymore. And it's not even a big deal. It's just a word.'

And she's like, 'why does everyone always go so deep and it's all fist in the air. If I want to be a proper rapper, if I want to be taken seriously – then I've got to say it how I want.'

She told me that they all say it. Nicky Minaj says it and she wants to be like her. She said us women need to show them that we're in the game too. Guys can spit bars – and they get respected. So the N word stays.

You keep asking me – I don't know when she's on. I'm not being weird... I just don't know.

Anyway, she says she's gonna say it. She doesn't care about their policy. She said freedom of speech is her right. There are people here who might sign her and she wants to stand out, be controversial.

So, er, well – the thing is, what Keisha said before – the 'fist in the air' thing? Well, that is me. I am one of those people.

Grows angry.

I don't think that just because you take away the 'er' part and add an 'a' it changes the history or the meaning. This is not what I'm about. Keisha knows I like writing, but she doesn't know what I write. She doesn't know that I'm trying to be 'in the game' too, but I'm trying to change it. I don't write aggressive lyrics. But about equality and love. She's gonna add the 'n' word to my words? My beautiful words.

Calms down.

So I, er, told the guy who signs you up. You know – where you write your name down if you wanna perform? I told him that Keisha is gonna say it. I told him and right now he's backstage telling her she can't go on.

I know there's people here who could sign you. You can really get noticed. So...er...the guy says I can go on instead.

So, it's me. I'm up next...

The Parisian Way

Stefanie Reynolds

> **A trainee solicitor realises how unfulfilled she is when she interviews a potential client. For ages 25 and above.**

So you have been in the country for *(looks at document)* five years. In this time, I can see you have opened your own bakery. *(Looks up at him.)* That's nice. And you came from? Sorry where are you from? Looks back at document. Oh! Paris! Lovely. OK... So you came to England four years ago? Some would argue why you would leave Paris to come to England!? *(Laughs to herself.)* But no. That's fair enough. Everyone has their journey and their life and their plan. Quite random but I was actually going to go to Paris. Isn't that funny? I was going to paint. Instead. But I decided to become a solicitor. And so here I am, a trainee solicitor and here you are, a handsome Parisian baker charged with *(looks down at document)* drunken disorderly behaviour and theft. What did you get me then!? *(Laughs.)* I'm kidding. I'm completely kidding. Just a little joke I like to have with all of my clients.

Now, the good news Mr Be-Cage?

Boocage?

Monsieur Boocage?

Boo-caj.

Thank you, Mr Beaucage. It sounds wonderful when you say it. Does it mean anything special? My name is Sarah. My parents wanted me to have the simplest, easiest name so I wouldn't have any difficulty in my life. Their words, not mine.

The good news is that because you were under the influence at the time of the robbery, you stand a better chance of – how long have you lived here for? *(Looks at file.)* Five years. That's great. That strengthens your case. Wow, it must be really exciting coming to a new country, learning a new language. I do envy you!

    Pause.

So, because you have been in the country just over five years and as this is your first offence we should reach a fair settlement. OK. I'm just going to start by asking you a few questions about the day of the incident. It's important to be as honest as possible.

    Pause.

I'm in my fifth year of training, if you can believe it! Five years. So in the five years that you've been here, you've set up a new life with new experiences and I've been in this office. *(Laughs.)* Isn't that funny!? You've moved to England, learnt a new language, opened your own business and I've been, here. Isn't that just incredible!?

    Pause.

Now, because this is your first offence we do have some options on how we want to –

Do you know what I do every morning? I arrive to work and I write a checklist of all the things I have to do that day and then I tick them off throughout the day. That's what I do. That's my life. Checklists. I've nearly finished my training now. And I've been given lots of responsibility, which is great. You know, my own cases. There are lots of social events on ran by the firm too, after work. Which is lovely. You know it's really nice of them. But I can't help but feel –

Mr Beaucage, do you ever feel as though you are stuck in one place and you have a heavy aching lump of guilt that you didn't go out and follow your dreams and do what you actually wanted to do?! I didn't imagine that this is where I would be. I thought I'd be out seeking adventure and – and experiences and love and sunshine and painting. I had all these plans, these big plans for myself, but here I am, in an office, ticking a checklist every morning, drinking coffee. I don't even like coffee. It's disgusting.

Pause. Maybe she is embarrassed.

I'm sorry. I can't do this. I have to – leave. I have to go to Paris. I have to learn French and live in Paris and live my life. Maybe I'll be *(speaks with French accent)* Sarah there.

Stands, ready to leave. Turns back to him.

Could I get your number? I might need some recommendations.

The Perfect Match

Olu Alakija

> An undercover detective fell in love with his
> target and got her pregnant. For ages 25 and
> above.

*Throughout the scene SAUL is pacing around his living
room and every now and then he stops and looks
through the net curtains onto his driveway, he is clearly
expecting someone. He adopts an English RP accent
when mimicking his boss.*

Why is this happening to me? Why now? This should
be the happiest day of my life and now it feels like
the worst... Sarah's gonna be back any minute now
and I still don't know what I'm gonna do... It wasn't
supposed to be like this... *(RP accent.)* 'We need you to
go undercover for a few weeks...a new deep surveillance
MI5 assignment...'* he said.

So now over a year later I'm stuck between a rock and
a very hard place... *'Your target is Sarah Saunders...she's
quite a looker...there's no such thing as getting too close...'*
He didn't exactly spell it out but I knew what he meant by
that... *'She's an animal rights extremist and these nutters
value animals over people. So, just pretend you like lovely,
little cuddly fluffy bunnies and we'll do the rest...'*

Pause.

Well I didn't have to pretend that I loved animals...
maybe that's the only thing that I have been honest
with her about...didn't plan on falling in love with her...so
kind, passionate, fiercely intelligent...the most amazing
smile...never met anyone quite like her...and no amount
of training could've prepared me for that...

> *Pause.*

*'We've been tracking her for years...algorithms, dating
history, childhood friends, favourite TV shows...you fit the
bill perfectly...you tick every single box.'*

He was right of course...we both lost our fathers at a
young age, we like the same music, same films and we
both have at least one parent that's not originally from
the UK...classic outsider syndrome...

I remember him joking that *'in some ways you're the
perfect match...'* if only he knew how true that is...and
now today of all days she tells me that she has some
amazing news...today when I'm supposed to be handing
in my report exposing her and all of her associates to
my boss.

> *Pause.*

The information I have in this file could lock her away for
ten years or more and God help me I don't know what
to do... She's pregnant...and I've wanted to be a father
for as long as I can remember but not like this... How can
I tell Sarah that our whole relationship is based on lies?

The Race
Mina Barber

> **An astronaut is to become the first black man on the moon. For ages 18 and above.**

A gym at the NASA training facility.

How about one photograph by the treadmill? Oh, you want me to go on it? Yeah, yeah sure.

> *MARK poses on the treadmill. It's as if the treadmill gets turned on at slow walking pace and MARK is a bit surprised.*

Whoa...you want me to do action shots as well? Of course no problem. So where d'you wanna start? I mean NASA, you feel like pinching yourself, d'you know what I mean...unusual stuff, like what? Space stuff?... OK, err... alright, you know when you go, like to the, you know... OK, when you take a dump, when you go to the, the John, you have to literally clamp yourself to the floor, like proper concrete boots, and it's not like a train toilet, it don't get flushed out into space, instead, get this, it gets freeze-packed and comes back to earth with you. My dad's a joker, he goes, 'So, you're gonna come back full of shit son?'

> *MARK laughs to himself but then realizes that the reporter isn't impressed and his laugh dies out.*

I guess it's not that funny... I mean that doesn't need to go in the article, right? Next question?... My parents, my dad's a mechanic from Havering. Havering's, best known for the BNP I guess, I wouldn't put that in. I always knew I wanted to work with machines, they're logical, you can see all their parts. Mechanics is in the family I guess, my dad's the one that started it all, took me to all the air shows. My mum?... She, erm, so, I wanted to ask about the title, for the article, my trainer said something about...

The treadmill speeds up slightly to a normal walking pace. MARK is taken by surprise.

What was I saying, yeah my dad he's been great, it's just me, and him. Alabama reminds me a bit of Havering, maybe that's not fair, I haven't left the base that much, it's like the army again. OK just a couple more... You wanna know a funny story about my parents?... Erm... well they used to get some funny looks when they picked me up from school, cos he's white and my mum, when she was alive, they even called my dad on her because they couldn't believe she was my mum. One woman goes to her, 'Are you the nanny?' My mum was so angry, proper vexed. That's not going in the article right? Yeah so about the title?

The treadmill speeds up now to a jog and MARK is caught unaware again.

No it's been excellent going round the schools, seeing their faces...yeah, you're right, I suppose they need to see people like them and of course I feel proud. I feel like Obama. No, no, don't put that in, sounds cheesy. 'I feel like Obama.' You like it? They asked some proper funny questions, like, 'Does ice cream melt in space?' and 'Do aliens have toys?' and, and 'If I fart in space, is it loud?' and, and 'Are there black people in space?' and I said that space is all black, well it's white as well, just not in between. There's no space in between... Look right, about the title?

The treadmill now speeds up to a run.

I don't think it's appropriate, it's not right, it's not correct, like technically not correct and I know the message is important, 'First Black Man on the Moon', but so is the truth, especially if we're going all the way out there, does it matter out there? Does that mean we have to carry our shit around forever? And it doesn't matter how fast you run, or how far you go. Your shit still comes back to earth with you. Of course I'm happy but I'm angry too, I'm angry that it's taken this long!

The treadmill suddenly stops and MARK looks into the distance as if the reporter is walking away.

No, I don't want to do this another time! Where are you going? Shit!

MARK is out of breath. Slight pause. He breathes in deeply.

'First Black Man on the Moon'...

The Right Representation

Karla Williams

A tragedy has taken place, and an employee is out to protect the company rather than the people. For ages 25 and above.

We'll take your case.
My fee is £700 per hour.
You can find a firm who'll charge less
But they can't do what we do.

We've spent the last ten years clearing up messes and
making law suits disappear.
We have contacts within the police, the media and the
courts.
You either spend your money with us and keep your
multi-million-pound company in business.
Or you don't stay in business.

With the Anderson case, the inquiry found the company
wasn't at fault.
It was the contractor who didn't properly maintain his
equipment and he was held responsible.
Karen Wilson PR made sure the press focused on the
contractor and not our client.
He ended up losing everything.
Should have spent more on his lawyers.

I see you own ten buildings with between twelve and thirty
flats each.

And all your buildings are private except this one.
Is this the only building that's had a fire?

Don't speak to the police until we get all our ducks in a row.
And don't speak to the press either.
We'll hold a press conference after you speak to the police.
I'll speak to Karen and make sure she handles it personally.
She can also bring up the possibility of blame being
placed elsewhere.
Her fee is in addition to ours.

I'll get my team to look in to the company that maintains
your buildings.
If we implicate them, then we can all pack up and go home.

We'll do everything we can to make sure it doesn't get
to this stage.
But how do you feel about making a pay out?
I'm not talking much – around the £150,000 mark.
That should be enough if the relatives of the victims
make a fuss.

Between you and me, I understand.
These people don't work, pay for nothing and want the
best of everything.
While you're losing money hand over fist, am I right?
I bet what the council gives you barely covers the
mortgage on that place.

Handouts help no one.
I've worked since the age of eleven. No one helped me
and looked what I've achieved.
People think we're helping them but we're not.
We're just enabling them to be lazy.

KARLA WILLIAMS

If more of these people lived within their means, the country
wouldn't be in the state it is.

This should be straightforward enough to make go away.
I'm not the youngest department head for no reason.
Give me a few weeks and let me do what I do best.
But you must do everything I tell you.
Listen to me and you'll be just fine.

The Thin Red Line

Olu Alakija

> **A police constable is guilt-ridden over his handling of disabled protestors. For ages 30 and above.**

MEM is a serving UK police constable standing in the office of his Sergeant and struggling to control his emotions as he speaks.

This isn't what I signed up for Sir. I used to love this job and as you know I've been awarded medals for bravery during my time in the force. If you want me on riot patrol I'm there...chase down a murder suspect...count me in... confront an armed terrorist...hold my non-alcoholic beer... but today for the first time since I put on this uniform nearly eleven years ago I felt physically sick wearing it...

   Pause.

How can I look my daughter in the eye tonight?

I already see far too little of her since our loss... God knows what I would do without her carer but how am I supposed to hug her today when I get back home with these hands...that I have had to use on people just like her in wheelchairs...people on crutches...women...the elderly?

   Pause.

They were just peacefully protesting about the government cuts for God's sake!

Pause.

Vulnerable people Sir who have had their disability benefits slashed...yet these hypocrites keep giving out dodgy deals to their rich friends... And keep filling their own fat faces with their expense accounts for duck ponds and suchlike...

Pause.

How can I answer Sinem tonight when she asks me *'How was work today Daddy? How many criminals did you catch today?'...'You make the world a safer place for everyone...you're my hero Daddy.'*

Pause.

Do I tell her that I was man-handling disabled people who were fighting for the rights of people like her? Pulling them from their wheelchairs and dragging them into the back of a police van? Me? Her father...the hero policeman?

Pause.

Not any more...not after today...brutalising the vulnerable for trying to protect their rights to a half decent life... well I guess I just found my red line...so I quit...I'm handing in my resignation Sir with immediate effect.

MEM begins to leave the office but turns back.

After my wife passed away I'm all my daughter has left... and I really want to go on being her hero for just a little while longer...

Tits

Rabiah Hussain

> **A young football player gets ready to tell her dad she doesn't want to be a girl anymore. For school ages.**

Tits. Yes, tits.
That's where the problem started.

She fidgets with her bra, indicating that it's uncomfortable.

It was OK to pretend they weren't there when they first started to...you know...emerge. But somewhere between the A cup and the C cup they became pretty hard to ignore. For the obvious reasons.

No matter how much I try to sleep on my stomach, to push down on my chest, they just won't stop...growing. And those stupid boys at school. I run to chase the football and instead of focusing on the target, they're too busy looking at...my targets. It doesn't help that I play centre forward.

And now... Well, Ds are pretty difficult to disguise. And when Mr Pratt told us that a scout for West Ham is coming to our next match on Monday, I made my decision in that moment. It's just time to let everyone else know.

Her alarm beeps. She looks at her watch.

One o'clock! Dad'll be here any minute. I run to mum's bedroom, climb over the bed, and get to the window, waiting to see his car pull up.

Pause.

Downstairs I can hear Mum banging plates around. She's in a huff because her new boyfriend Steve, doesn't like Dad staying. But whatever anyone's mood tonight, I have to tell them.

Pause. She runs back to the window.

Dad's pulling into the driveway! Oh God. I feel nervous. OK, OK. Usually I would be so excited; I'd jump from the top stair down to the bottom and run to him. But today, my nerves are getting the better of me. Damon, my younger brother, is already outside running around in excitement. Idiot.

Dad's taking something out of the boot. And he has...a football! Sick! Yes! Another to add to my... Dad gives the football to Damon.

She stops abruptly.

He looks up and sees me. Gives me that big smile he always does. Then he holds up a... Claire's bag. I'm guessing my present isn't football boots.

Pause.

I can hear everyone at the door. I walk out of the room, towards the stairs. I'm trying to walk downstairs but my feet don't seem to want to move anymore. Mum is hugging dad whilst Damon hangs off his leg. Steve shakes his hand coldly and I just watch them. Dad notices me standing there at the top of the stairs. I think I'm going to be sick.

They all turn to look at me. Waiting for me to run to Dad. But I can't seem to. The burden of my body – my tits – seem to be holding me back. I sit down on the top step and watch as their faces change, knowing that there's something wrong. I try to talk but my tongue is heavy.

Pause. She takes a long, deep breath.

I put my hand under my top and reach around to the back. I unhook my bra, and slide the straps down my arms, like I've learnt to. I feel a freedom as my tits start to hang down. I pull my bra out from under my t-shirt and throw it down. Everyone's questioning eyes are burning into me. I take a deep breath and... 'I want to change. I don't want to be a girl anymore.'

Twisted Tarot

Shai Hussain

> **A tarot reader gives advice to a customer with whom she shares something in common. For ages 18 and above.**

MURIELA sits in a yoga pose when she realises that she has a customer. She has a thick mystic accent.

Oh. Hello. Do come in. What would you like to explore today?

Love? But of course.

MURIELA closes her eyes.

I see that you are happy, content with the man that you are with. But worry that he may be leading you...astray.

MURIELA opens her eyes.

I'm sorry? Do I think he's leading you astray? I can't tell for sure. All I can say is what the spirits tell me. Maybe we'll have better luck with these.

MURIELA takes out a pack of tarot cards and shuffles them.

Remember, whatever the spirits tell me, there's always room for error. Oh yes, fate is completely predestined, there's nothing you can do to change that. But sometimes fate can be read wrong. Nothing to worry about, madam.

She lays three cards down on the table.

The first card will tell us how far the souls of you and your partner have come in your journey.

She turns over the card, hurt by what she sees. She closes her eyes again.

You've shared a wonderful life together. You've never attempted to get in the way of his dreams, despite the way he has challenged yours. He has challenged yours a lot. But you've never given up hope on one another.

But that is the past.

She flips over the second card.

No, no, please don't be afraid of the skeletons. The card may look bad, but it's all about interpretation. It shows that you're currently going through challenges, and you're braving the storm, fighting with all your might and...

MURIELA closes her eyes.

Your child is hurting. There is much pain at home. Much anger. An emptiness that eats away at...that eats away at –

MURIELA breaks out of her mystic accent. She's a cockney.

I can't do this.

I'm sorry. You know why. I know you know.

Don't make me do this, please don't make – *I love him too!*

I can't give him back. I just can't. Mate, he's made me feel more complete than I've ever felt in my whole life. He – he told me he's happier with me. He told me he's going to leave you.

Got a better idea. Let's let the spirits decide. This card here tells us how the future of your relationship looks. I'll prove it to you. He'll leave you and come to me. You wanted to know? Let's see how this ends *right now!*

MURIELA hesitantly turns over the last card.

Bah! What do the spirits know?

VV

Mahad Ali

> **A girl has a crush, but the problem is, he's a character in a comic book. For school ages.**

VV is in the toilets, she has been crying and is drying her eyes.

Why do girls do that, when they see you are happy, try to ruin it for you? I knew I should've kept it to myself, I'm so stupid!

But Amanda just kept on asking, you seeing anyone? Got a crush on anyone? Come on there must be someone?... So I told her, just to shut her up... Oh he's Japanese that's strange; I didn't know there were any Japanese people in England...she's so ignorant!

But when she called call me weird I almost lost it! This was coming from a girl who admitted to having a crush on Alan Sugar. Yes Alan Sugar! That fossil in a suit that goes around telling people you're fired on *The Apprentice*! But I didn't make fun of her even though I wanted to retch; grab a bucket to vomit in disgust. I kept my thoughts to myself.

> *VV brings out a comic strip and is viewing a specific picture in it.*

You see that's why I love Kyoya, he accepts you for who you are. He is the most intelligent person I know. He is usually calm and reserved. While he can occasionally be strict, he is respected by almost everyone. He tolerates weirdness and never gets angry, even when I'm being my sarcastic self!

I don't care if she doesn't think he's cool. His level-headedness, wit, and rimless glasses are cool to me!

Sure he amuses himself by teasing me about my short hair and being a bit awkward but we share a friendship based on mutual respect for each other.

She puts down the comic book in frustration.

He says that while he is interested in me, he doesn't feel like he deserves me and that out of respect for me he would never... He's harsh at times but says it's for my own good, that it keeps things clear between us.

She picks up the comic book again and stares at the picture of Kyoya.

But it's hard to take not being able to connect with him in the way I want...it's not so easy getting over something like this.

Maybe Amanda's right, maybe I am weird and need to live in the real world! But it's hard giving up what you know. When my dad stopped smoking he said he just did cold turkey. I said I don't understand? He said that it means giving up an addiction, on the spot. But I'm not addicted am I?

VV closes the comic book.

Maybe I am just a little but it's helped me through difficult times.

But I'm gonna give it a try...no more Kyoya...no more anime.

>   *She places the comic book on the floor and walks
>   away.*

Watching

Karla Williams

Watching people through binoculars becomes a pastime for a neighbour until they witness a domestic violence incident. For ages 18 and above.

She stands with a pair of binoculars.

22.29 and 56 seconds
57
58
59
Ten thirty.

I can always rely on Mr and Mrs Jackson.
Friday night takeaway,
he falls asleep in front of the TV,
and then up to your separate bedrooms at 10.30 sharp.
Their life's worse than mine.
Mum's always on at me to get married,
but fuck getting married if that's what you become.

Dennis is drunk – surprise, surprise.
Every night he gets pissed.
Why Melanie puts up with him I have no idea – fucking waste of space.
What does he even do apart from drink and pass out?
Here she comes, pissed off as usual...
Oh she slapped him!

Peter's home tonight.
He's never home this early,
especially on Fridays.
And he's got another one;
some insecure bitch with daddy issues.
Are they...?
On my God they are!
Why hasn't he drawn the curtains?
He normally draws the curtains!

    Stares intently.

No, no don't close them.
Leave them open.
Leave them open!

    Annoyed.

Thanks for ruining my night number twenty-five!
Did you know you were the twenty-fifth woman he's
brought back to his flat?!
I've been waiting ages to watch him fuck one.
Thanks a lot!

    Sighs.

Dennis looks so scary when he's angry.
What's he gonna do this time: shout back at her, push
her, leave?
Oh shit.
He hit her.
He's never hit her that hard before.
Oh my God!
Is she,
is she moving?

KARLA WILLIAMS

She's not moving...
Is that blood?

Covers her mouth in shock.

Where is he going?
Why is he in the front garden?
Leave the car and get back to your wife!
Call an ambulance you idiot?!
Shit...
Is he looking at me?
He's seen me!

Panicked.

What am I gonna do?
Oh shit!
What am I gonna do?

Should I hide?
But he's already seen me.
What should I do?
What should I *do*?!

Just ignore it
He'll go away.
Pretend you don't hear it and he'll go away.

Mum?
No, mum – leave it.
I said leave it.
Don't answer the door!

Welcome To The Good Life

Bisola Elizabeth Alabi

> An office worker hopes that none of her colleagues know that she is living in her car. Age stated in monologue as 25 years old.

EMILY DAVIDSON, twenty-five years old, is now living in her car and wearing a nightgown over her work clothes. There's a knock on the window, it's her work colleague Tom.

Tooooooommm. Oh my Gooooóod, what brings you here? I was just having a quick nap, yeah in my car, wearing my PJs before I... Well funny thing is before I took a nap I just had a Pot Noodle and you know how it gets all messy when your slurping and chewing, so I didn't want to get any of it on my clothes.

Beat.

Anyway enough about me, how's Ruth and the kids? Yeah...just ignore the boxes and the hangers with my... bras on them. I'm giving them away to the charity shop. You know the one, Trade? You've never heard of Trade? Very high-end charity shop way better than the Salvation Army, nothing wrong with them but you can't beat Trade. That was where I was *actually* going...before you showed up.

Beat.

Seriously... I promise you I'm fine please stop asking me. In fact what are you doing here? This doesn't seem like your type of scene. I see you more as a Shoreditch hipster; sorry I shouldn't judge...*we* shouldn't judge a book by its cover.

Beat.

Sorry... I'm sorry Tom I just need you to...

Beat.

Please...please don't tell anyone that you've seen me here. Especially Julie, I'm already on my last warning. I've been in worse situations, people have underestimated me all my life and I've proven them wrong. Every. Single. Time.

Beat.

What's that in your hand? A whip round? I don't want it, keep it. Oh my God, how long have you all known? Does Julie know? Have all of you been talking about me behind my back, like I'm some charity case? You all knew how I was (living)... I don't want your pity please I can't stomach it. I can't bear you looking at me like that. Please can you go, just pretend that you never saw me. Please. I'm sorry, please just leave.

What Can I Do For You?

Shai Hussain

> **A fast food server is given the chance to win a lot of money. For ages 18 and above.**

Slides the window open. A smile as wide as the ocean, BENSON is customer service to perfection.

Welcome to Burger Daddy. What can I do for you? Would you like to make that a meal deal for an extra £1.30? No pressure, but it's worth it.

> *Big grin.*

Perfect. If you drive forward to the next window we'll get your food for you as soon as we can. Have a nice day!

> *As the car drives off, BENSON's smile follows and fades as it reaches the next window. After a pause, BENSON turns forward to greet the next customer with his trademark smile.*

Welcome to Burger Daddy. What can I do for you? I'm sorry? What can you do for me? That's not quite how this works, madam. Would you like to try our new Chilli Chicken Daddy? It's really got what I call the 'Beijing Zing!'

> *The customer shows BENSON a big wad of cash.*

Wow. How much money is – That's a lot of Beijing Zing. Is that for me?

BENSON's face drops.

Ninety seconds to convince you that it is? Why? Of course
I want it!
You're really putting me on the spot here. Have we started
already or – Um... OK. Well...come on, ninety seconds?
Eighty-two!?
OK, well I'm working here. Obviously I need the money...

The customer makes a move to drive away.

Whoa whoa madam, wait! I – I – I deserve this money, madam!

I'm a good guy. I'm not perfect, nobody is, but I sure as
hell know that I'm better than most of the people in this
world. OK, I don't know that for sure, maybe I've just met
the wrong people but...oh, I'm wasting time...

Look. As far as I can see it, money controls everything.
And the world is so rigged that the only way you get it
is if you're born into it, or you're ready to play the game.
If you're born with it, you get your private schools, your
tuition fees paid and then once you graduate, friends of
daddy, do daddy a favour and get you a paid internship at
their investment banking firm. And given you don't mess
it up, you're made for life and hand it down to your own
kids and the loop goes on.

Or you don't get that privilege, and you play the game.
Your only way to the top is by bringing everyone else
down. It's like you need to mute your guilt, be done with
your ethics. Love nobody and your enemies have nothing
to threaten you with. Tell me that you made that money
fair and square, madam, honestly and truly? Cheat, lie,
steal – keep your eye on the prize.

Privilege wasn't handed to me, madam. I play the game too, but I've never had it in me to bend the rules, let alone break them. My Aunt Christina taught me that the way to happiness was through respect, honesty, discipline. But what's it got me? Heartbreak. A shared-living rat-infested bedsit. And a side order of fries. Aunt Christina followed the rules too. And what did she get?

Brought her over here for better medical treatment. The way her eyes lit up when we had a Big Ben selfie, you should've seen it. But apparently, medical treatment isn't free for people like her.

'Temporary visitor from a non-European country'. That's what the NHS calls her. Ridiculous. Not one doctor ready to save the life of this sweet, sweet mother who's never hurt a fly. 'Temporary visitor from a non-European–' That's my Aunt Christina! I'm here, working towards paying medical tuition fees just so when there's some other guy with a dying mother who's a 'temporary visitor from a non-European country', I can do something.

I can tell by the look in your eyes that you don't believe me. And you know something? I don't care. Because in the grand scheme of things – money, power, politics – none of that stands a chance against cancer.

The customer hands over the cash.

Are you sure?

BENSON takes it. Once the customer has driven off, BENSON beams with delight.

Mute your guilt, be done with your ethics. Keep your eye on the prize, baby!

Why I Love R. Kelly

Abraham Adeyemi

> **A school girl defends her reasons for loving R. Kelly. Age stated in monologue as 15 years old.**

AALIYAH, fifteen, black, Brummy. She sits on the floor with a notepad and a pencil in her lap and intermittently sketches throughout. She is behind the school bike shed overseeing the school fields.

(She sings the chorus of R. Kelly's 'Ignition', whilst drawing.) ... Ayyyyyyy!

> *Pause.*

Let me tell you why I love R. Kelly. I love R. Kelly because R. Kelly lov... – R. Kelly loved – Aaliyah. And I mean, what is there not to love about people called Aaliyah?

> *Pause.*

That Aaliyah. *(Points at herself confidently.)* Nah, THIS Aaliyah.

Hmm... Bit controversial, init? When I first started school, people used to make jokes, say R. Kelly's gonna come get me, and –

> *She pulls a revolted face.*

And that was before people even knew I was a fan.
Everyone always say it's weird, that I love him so much.
They don't get it. They can't get it.

Pause.

I know it's nasty. Like, fifteen! Married her at fifteen,
what the hell, that's my age and then everything
else, the young girls... But then, actually, some places
that'd be alright you know. Like some of them Muslim
countries.

Pause.

But it's not just the Muslims. Like, if you go to Brazil
you can have sex at fourteen, fourteen in Italy, fifteen in
France and – oh my God – twelve in the Philippines and
Angola.

Pause.

Don't ask me why I know that.

She gives an awkward look.

Anyway, none of that matters, because he's never been
found guilty. And even if he was... I... Would still love him.

Pause.

It's not like you lot don't still love Chris Brown, we're all
hypocrites ain't we... See, it's possible to just love someone
for what they're good at... To separate them from their
fuckeries... And I need to. I need to love R. Kelly...

Silence.

Anyway. You know the meaning of Aaliyah?

She begins to roll up a spliff.

Ascending.

She takes a draw from a spliff.

Silence.

Ascending. Ascen... Shit.

She quickly puts the spliff out of sight and excessively sprays perfume.

(Fake smile.) Hi miss!

She waits a moment, rolls her eyes then brings the spliff back out and takes a draw. She starts to sketch.

They just go together, you know. It's like, my mind is free. Like it can't be stopped, it just forgets everything...

She sighs heavily.

Bet the head's snooty PA's gonna lift her head above the screen soon, notice I'm gone. Bet she's just on Facebook all day, how hard can it really be. Maybe if they'd noticed sooner, we wouldn't be here.

Pause.

He doesn't even know who I am, there's like what, one thousand five hundred-ish kids here. I've never spoken to him. Never been in trouble. Or top of the class.

Pause.

I've been skiving, init. Missing school. I've decided I'm not doing this no more. It's not for me. So even if that's what this meeting's about, them telling me I'm gone, guess what? I don't care because I wanna be gone anyway.

Silence.

Let me tell you why I love R. Kelly.

Pause.

I love R. Kelly because he made me believe I can fly. *(Sniggers.)* He made me believe that I could be great, no matter what. And I really believed it... I still believe it.

Silence.

Let me tell you why I really love R. Kelly.

She takes a long draw from a spliff.

I... I love R. Kelly because, I'm like him.

Pause.

I'm like him. My friends don't really know. Not properly. But the school does. It took them a while... I was smart. Well, not proper smart. My kind of smart. Crafty.

Pause.

Copying homework. Or getting into school like suuuuuuuper early. Like, caretakers early. Six a.m. in the morning early. Because there's always a teacher who needs to be in school early.

Pause.

And I'd make for the reprographics room. And that's all there was to it. I take what I need. The exam papers. And leave. But it wasn't long until... I got it wrong. Because just as I was walking out...

She sketches.

Everybody says I'm good at it, and if you know what you're good at, it only makes sense to focus on that and be the very best you can be at it, right?

Pause.

Being like, really really really good at one thing can be enough, can't it?

Silence.

Well... I'm gonna find out. One way or another. Just me, my dollar and a dream!

She laughs uneasily.

School's never want that though. They just want you to know how to pass exams and in all the right subjects. No matter what your strengths are. If it ain't like the proper academic stuff... Then they don't care, not really. Apparently that's what gets them up the league tables.

Silence.

I was never the loud one. The boisterous one. I was always the 'don't have to worry about her because she behaves herself and keeps quiet' one, and 'even if she doesn't contribute in class, she gets by alright and we have too much grief with the naughty kids' one.

Pause.

That's why it took them a while. And they say they're trying to help me, help me for the real world... But I can't be helped. Like, I can't.

Silence.

I'm not a bad person. I'm not a bad child. I never wanted to be like this. If I could...

Pause.

But I've needed, and still need, help and who better to help me but me to help myself? Because they don't know the help I need, they're not giving me the help I need. They're not listening to me, to what I need.

Pause.

Stealing exam papers. That's what I'd do. Help me. I'd type all the words into the computer and make the computer read it to me. Our little secret. Next step? Memorise as many word patterns as I could, and letters and stuff.

Pause.

It's not as complicated as it sounds.

Silence.

It used to be calling in sick. Pretending my period was

killing. Forgot my glasses. Feeling dizzy. Just any excuse whatsoever.

Pause.

When you're one of the good kids, everybody believes you. They don't question anything. Well, now they will.

Silence.

Fuck it. They can get rid of me. I don't need this shit, I've got this far, they can go to hell, I don't need to explain myself. Because they're never gonna be able to fix me. I'm always gonna be like this.

Pause.

I love R. Kelly, because I'm like him and I need him. Because, you see, if I can't love R. Kelly, and believe in him the way I do... I can't believe in me. I can't believe that I can do this. Life.

Pause.

I'm like R. Kelly. I can't read. I can't write. And, with all my might, I've made sure that nobody has ever realised my plight.

Pause.

And I don't need to. Look at him. He's a genius. He used what he had, and made the best of it. That's what I'm gonna do...

Pause.

So sorry if I won't join you in condemning him. Sorry if I don't see a monster like you insist I should.

Pause.

Because if R. Kelly can't read or write, yet have achieved so much in his own right, who's to say that I don't have the right – despite all – to believe I can fly with all my might?